READ THE ROAD SIGNS

MEREDA CRUZ

Copyright © 2016 Mereda Cruz.

All rights reserved. No part of this book may be reproduced, stored, or transmitted by any means—whether auditory, graphic, mechanical, or electronic—without written permission of both publisher and author, except in the case of brief excerpts used in critical articles and reviews. Unauthorized reproduction of any part of this work is illegal and is punishable by law.

ISBN: 978-1-4834-5403-0 (sc)
ISBN: 978-1-4834-5402-3 (e)

Library of Congress Control Number: 2016913980

Because of the dynamic nature of the Internet, any web addresses or links contained in this book may have changed since publication and may no longer be valid. The views expressed in this work are solely those of the author and do not necessarily reflect the views of the publisher, and the publisher hereby disclaims any responsibility for them.

Any people depicted in stock imagery provided by Thinkstock are models, and such images are being used for illustrative purposes only.
Certain stock imagery © Thinkstock.

Lulu Publishing Services rev. date: 8/29/2016

For my my son, Ben;
my mother and father;
my niece, Heidi who encouraged me to write it;
my two best friends, Pamela and Jane, who
have been there for the journey;
and every one of my seven siblings:
Robert, Kirsten, Kathryn, Ingrid, Peter, Simone, and Krystle.

CONTENTS

Acknowledgments xi
Introduction xiii
Being Single 1
Frankenstein's Concept 3
Selling Your House 7
Invest in Your Inner Self 10
Observe What You Attract 15
The Empty Basket Concept 17
Living in Reverse 20
Have a Destination 22
Don't Look for Bread in the Meat Aisle 25
Helpful Guidelines 26
    Number One 26
    Number Two 27
    Number Three 27
    Number Four 27
    Number Five 28
    Number Six 29
    Number Seven 30
Get the Right Exposure 31
Never Conform 33
Are You Choosing between Two Guys? 35
Don't Buy a House without Viewing It 36

Always Go with Your Instinct	39
Actions Speak Louder than Words	40
Be a Friend to Yourself	42
Be a Friend to Others	43
The Supply Teacher	44
The Pied Piper	46
Climb the Hill or Take the Flat Route?	48
Teacup Ride or Roller Coaster?	50
The Power of No Reply	53
Leading Lady or Chorus	56
Think like a Ten	61
Empty Restaurant Concept	63
Money Doesn't Make You Better	66
Don't Show the Whole Film, Only the Trailer	68
Tennis Game	70
Never Show Your Hand	72
The Ballerina Concept	74
Never Give Up Your Life for a Man	76
Monkey See, Monkey Do	77
Flip the Coin	78
Beauty Is in the Eye of the Beholder	80
Fallback Girl	82
Limbo Land	83
Indicate, Mirror, Signal, Manoeuvre	85
Unplug the Source	87
A Good Gambler Knows When to Quit	88
Reason, Season, or Lifetime?	90
Red Wolf	91
Living in the Moment	93
The Emperor's New Clothes	*95*
Do We Ever Really Know Someone?	97
Life Is Short	99
Find the Right Receptor	100

Does He Have Your Manual? 101
If You Look Too Hard, You Don't Find It 102
What Book Are You? 103
True Love Does Exist 104
What Do Men Really Want in a Woman? 106
Women Need to Stick Together 108
Worzel Gummidge *109*
It's Okay to Be Single 111
Cinderella Slipper 113
Never Show a Man You Feel Threatened by Another Woman 115
Why Doesn't He Reply? 118
Wax and Polish 119
The Big R 121
Don't Fish with a Fish on the End of Your Rod 123
Don't Let Them Put You in a Box 125
Own It 127
Personal Date Night 128
Dress Yourself Top to Toe in Self-Esteem 131
The Checklist 132
Conclusion 145
About the Author 147

ACKNOWLEDGMENTS

I would like to thank many people for inspiring me to write this book. My father was an incredibly intelligent man. He had many script ideas but never did anything about them. I guess, through him, I learned a valuable lesson. Take action. While you're thinking about it, someone else *is* doing it—someone else is living your dream, turning your dreams into reality.

I have to thank my niece Heidi, who encouraged me to write this book; she is my little twin. She is a polisher and makes everyone shine.

I would like to thank my sister Simone who allowed me to share some of her experiences and who has been there all the way to support me.

My friend Pamela and I have laughed for hours about our dating lives. She is a truly beautiful person and funny without knowing it. My friend Jane has shared countless stories with me, and we have laughed until we cried about life and dating. Both Pamela and Jane are friends who I will count on my hand at the end of my life as true friends. I feel blessed to have found them.

I would like to thank all the people who have opened up to me and shared their intimate stories. For obvious reasons I can't name you, but you know who you are. I loved listening to your experiences. Hopefully, they will inspire others.

I would like to thank Dean, who has been a true friend and an amazing stepfather to my son. Ben is blessed to have you in his life, and you will make an amazing dad one day.

I want to thank my son, who is the reason for everything.

Thank you to all my family, especially my sister Kathryn, who is the most selfless person I know; my sister Krystle, who inspired my front cover; and Angela, who moved next door when we were kids and is part of the family.

Finally, I want to thank my eccentric parents, who gave me a beautiful mind.

INTRODUCTION

Have you ever been driving down the motorway lost in your own thoughts, and missed your exit? It can add another half an hour to your journey.

Missing a road sign has happened to us all at one time or another. This relates to the signs we receive in life; if you don't read the road signs, you can sometimes lose years of your life. The message is "pay attention." When unwelcome experiences have knocked on the door, when we look back, there were probably numerous signs that we just didn't read or, more importantly, simply ignored.

I have used the metaphor of the motorway to represent the importance of not wasting years of your life with the wrong man. Don't ignore the signs that your relationship is in need of attention. Don't stay on the same journey when it no longer serves you. Change gears or change direction, but, most of all, be present and pay attention to the signposts in life—they are there every day.

I was inspired to write this book for a number of reasons. The most significant was an experience I had when someone very close to me had an emotional breakdown. This person was beautiful, intelligent, and successful. She owned two houses with her partner of ten years and, to the outside world, appeared to have the perfect life. But the perfect show that she presented was a facade. The doors were opened when her relationship broke down and the truth came out. She had suffered many years of domestic abuse. Her partner had continuously chipped away at her self-esteem and made her feel like she wasn't good enough for him. He criticised her hair, her weight, and her sense of humour. He would come home in the early hours of the morning without an explanation as to where he had been, which progressed from staying out late to not returning home at all.

It transpired that he had been living a double life and was active on many dating sites. When this finally unfolded, my friend became a complete wreck. She was emotionally unstable, which resulted in her having to resign from her job. She was left with nothing: no house, no money, and what seemed like no future ahead of her. She turned up on my doorstep with a bag of clothes, tears streaming down her face, devastated that the man she had spent ten years of her life with had been having an affair and had literally taken her life away from her. The saddest part was that even though she had known that the relationship was toxic and damaging for her health, she couldn't remove herself from the situation. She had allowed herself to continue in those torturous circumstances because she couldn't see a way out. She had completely lost all control, and the only reason she had finally broken free was because he had left her for someone else. It was at that moment that I vowed I would do everything in my power to prevent anyone close to me from having to endure anything like that again. I did everything I could to help build her life back together. Today, she is completely transformed. She has started her own business and met the love of her life.

This is just one example of many that I will share in the pages of this book. I hope that sharing these experiences will benefit other women—women who can learn from the misfortunes of myself, my friends, my family, and many others who I have met along the way. I hope to prevent people from ever having to feel the way I and others have felt and to teach people how to recognise bad situations before they find themselves living in them, trying to figure a way out.

Since I was a young child, I have found myself providing analogies to people to explain the complexities of life. These have manifested into simple and understandable concepts, which I have used in all areas of my life. I have compiled these concepts into this book in the hope that people can relate to them as I have. These concepts are demonstrated using examples from my life experiences and the life experiences of others. My greatest wish is that you can learn from them.

I have spent the last fourteen years working predominately with men. I have spent many ten-hour shifts traveling in a van with men, sometimes being the only female, and I have observed them, listened to them, and, more importantly, learned from them: how they think and what makes them tick. I listened to their endless stories, thinking that if only the girl had done this or done that, she could have changed the dynamics of her relationship without question.

The pinnacle moment, when I decided to finally put pen to paper, was during a night in with the girls. I sat among a group of friends who were beautiful, intelligent, and independent women. Some were married; some were currently dating; and some were single. I listened to stories of their affairs, which were tales of woe—being with the wrong man, being messed around by a man, or desperately trying to find a man.

One of the girls told us about a guy she had recently met and had had lunch with. She was explaining how excited she was about her upcoming second date when one of my friends said, "Oh no, stay away from him. He is a player! You will only get hurt."

This annoyed me. My friend was a good catch. She was funny, great company, and intelligent. Why should she have to be worried? It was implied he had the upper hand, but we were all equals, weren't we?

From that night forward, I vowed to do all I could to empower women to call the shots in their relationships. I was sick of wiping my friends' tears, sick of going on dates myself and feeling disappointment. I was sick of watching my friends and family settle with the wrong man or grab the first guy who showed them interest, either out of insecurity and panic that they would be left on the shelf or, even worse, because they just didn't want be alone.

My own personal experiences are incorporated into this book—how I was received as a single person both at work and in social circles. I hope these examples will empower the single girl who is sitting on her sofa right now and wondering if this is as good as it gets. I hope my experiences and these concepts will inspire and motivate her and others who are single or in need of a little guidance—and provide help with a lighthearted flavour that will allow each reader to smile, laugh, and learn.

BEING SINGLE

I am guessing that if you have bought my book you are recently single, have been single for a while, or are thinking about becoming single. I can empathise with you.

If you are newly single you have probably talked endlessly about your ex to your friends, and they are probably fed up with hearing your ex's name. Singing love songs full volume on the way to work, you come home to an empty house. At bedtime you look over at the empty space next to you. You have spent hours looking through old pictures of when you first met your ex and then looking at new pictures posted on social media of your ex with a new partner, convincing yourself that they really aren't all that. Yes, we have all been where you are sitting right now.

The next stage is the recovery. You may browse the self-help aisle in the bookstore, looking for inspiration, making excuses to the cashier as to why you are in the self-help section! Most people have been there at one time or another. It may be that you are in a good place but in need of a little dating advice. Being single after a long-term relationship can be a daunting experience. When that is coupled with the possibility of having to sell your home or lose mutual friends and family, it is a huge hurdle to overcome.

It is my sincere belief that you will take something from this book, and by the time you get to the end, I hope you will feel a little better about being single. If you are nursing a broken heart, take comfort in knowing that millions of people across the world have had broken hearts at one time or another, including me. One thing is certain—you will get over it. It's your choice: embrace this new period in your life or keep living in the past.

In this book, I will remind you of the reasons why staying in the wrong relationship is far worse than being alone. I will explore why we gravitate toward certain types of relationships, and I will offer some tips for when you are back in the dating game.

So grab yourself a coffee, and get comfortable.

FRANKENSTEIN'S CONCEPT

The famous story of Frankenstein's monster is one we are all familiar with. Victor Frankenstein hopes to bring the dead back to life and ends up creating a monster. The moral of the story is this: when something is dead, let it go.

I relate that message to relationships. It's a simple principle I live by. Have you ever been in a relationship where there has been infidelity? Some people can work through it. However, for the majority, it damages the relationship beyond repair. The betrayal can breed insecurity, which creates anxiety and panic that were not present before. For example, if your unfaithful partner receives a text late at night, you automatically feel sick. You don't want to challenge him because you said you wouldn't mention it, and you are trying to move forward. And yet you desperately want to check his phone and ask who the sender was. The thought of what it might be—what it might mean—eats away at you, and you become anxious and stressed. Then the heated arguments begin, and the pain is resurrected. Infidelity is just one example of many that can contribute to the breakdown of a relationship.

When we try to revive something that is dead, we create a monster. We become two people engaging from a different place—one may feel anger and resentment and the other feels frustration as they're trying to rebuild the damage that has been caused within the relationship. This seldom works, and we have to let go. When we have tried everything, it's simply time to move on. As with Dr. Frankenstein, do you want to remember the relationship you had or create a monster out of the relationship you are desperately clinging to? If you are still living in the last chapter, how can you start a new one?

An example of this comes from one of my friends. She was with the man of her dreams—or so she thought. He appeared to be the perfect guy. One day, for no apparent reason, she picked up his phone when he went to the shop. She had never looked at his phone before, but, for some reason, that day she did. There was a message to his ex-girlfriend saying, "I miss your face," and numerous other messages. He wasn't just in contact with her; he had been seeing her for the past three years, living a double life!

After the initial shock and weeks of living apart, with him begging for forgiveness, she decided to take him back. But the relationship didn't work; she had become insecure and paranoid. She didn't want him to go out with his male friends, and she kept checking his phone. The infidelity had created a monster in her. They stayed together for two more years, which were horrible. She spent her days filled with anger, bitterness, and resentment toward him, feeling that he had caused her to become a different person.

Another friend of mine went through a very difficult time toward the latter end of her relationship. After finding out that her partner had been seeing another woman, her physical and mental health took a turn for the worse. She went from a healthy size twelve to a size six. She had trust issues, and when her partner went to work she would follow him. Her days were filled with anxiety and panic. When his phone went off, she felt sick with worry. When he went out with his friends, she spent the evening stressing about what he was doing. The relationship became toxic. The infidelity had knocked her confidence so much that she remained with him, even when she learned that he was still seeing the other woman. I watched him blame her for the infidelity and make her believe it was her fault. It was alarming to see the effect that one person can have on another's mental health. The relationship became so bad that she was barely sleeping. This is a classic example of Frankenstein's concept. This was no longer a healthy relationship; my friend was a prisoner of her own making. Eventually, violence started, and the rows became so nasty that he started pushing her during arguments, which resulted in the police being involved.

When a relationship is over, it is important to let go and remove yourself. I have seen other relationships turn violent when people have remained together when they should have walked away. The partners they knew were not there anymore, and monsters were created in both people. It does happen.

Domestic violence is a global issue. I have seen it firsthand on numerous occasions. Even with couples who have never resorted to violence, emotions can take over, and bad things can happen. Remember this if you are ever involved in something similar.

Frankenstein's concept is no way to live, are you in a relationship that has turned you into a monster?

"Don't stay in a relationship which has turned you into a monster."

SELLING YOUR HOUSE

Have you ever sold something important, like a house or a car? Before most of us would allow viewings of our home, we would clean the house, polish the mirrors, and have the aroma of fresh coffee wafting throughout the house. If a bathroom tile was cracked, most of us would fix it.

In your life, *you* are your most valuable asset—so why not invest in yourself? We don't think twice about paying for a new kitchen or new bathroom, but we sometimes forget that it's important to invest in ourselves. If you're not happy with your hair, change it; try a new hairstyle or a different colour. If you don't like your teeth, see what you can do to change them. Money may be a barrier for some things, but a haircut and a few new clothes can do wonders for your confidence. If you want something bad enough, you will find a way. I wasn't happy with my teeth, so I did something about it, and it was the best money I have ever spent.

If you are dating, you are essentially putting yourself up for sale. Is it time for a new you?

Do you feel that your look could do with a little help? If you aren't very good at putting on makeup, visit a makeup counter. Most name brands offer free makeovers. Makeup and clothes can transform people. If you aren't very good with clothes, ask someone who is. There are certain clothes that will enhance your body shape, and certain colours will complement you more than others. Make it a fun day out with friends; the results can be incredible. A friend of mine always wore baggy clothes and didn't experiment much with makeup. With a little help, she experimented with different looks and now feels excited about getting ready to go out. This, in turn, increased her confidence. If you look good, you feel good.

Another good example of this is a friend of mine who had lost her shapely bust after having her first child. This really bothered her. When she was dating, she would talk to me for hours about how she dreaded being intimate because she wasn't happy with her body. For some women, this would not affect them at all, but we are all individuals, and this affected my friend's confidence. Her body had changed, and she just wasn't happy with it. My friend would only be intimate when wearing her bra, and this had a huge impact on her sex life. After much discussion, she decided to invest in breast augmentation. She was over the moon with the results, and she felt that it transformed her life.

Another friend of mine had the opposite problem: she had very large breasts, which caused severe backaches. Although she was slim, she would struggle to buy clothes that would fit her body shape. After saving for a long time, she took the plunge and had a reduction procedure.

I appreciate the fact that surgery is not for everyone, but I am a strong believer in investing in yourself. If you add up how much you spend on makeup and clothes throughout a year, it can be very pricey. It's all about the bigger picture, and money spent now might make every day in the future a little bit better. For some, investing in a gym or personal trainer will be the right choice, for getting fit and taking pride in your appearance promotes self-worth, which equates to feeling better about yourself.

Another way to invest in yourself is to sign up for that course you have always wanted to take or to learn that language you've always been interested in. It may be you've always wanted to learn to dance or learn a new sport. These are fantastic ways to meet new people while you are investing in yourself. Let the focus be on you, and do something for yourself.

I remember the first pair of expensive sunglasses I bought. They were my pride and joy. I didn't leave them on a sun lounger or misplace them, which I did with the cheaper pairs I bought. Think for a few moments about what your most prized material possession is. Think about how well you look after it, enjoy it, and respect it. As I have said before, you are your most valuable asset, so why don't you give the same respect to yourself that you do for your most prize possession? It's something to think about. Do you value yourself?

INVEST IN YOUR INNER SELF

As I've explained, *you* are your most valuable asset, so invest in yourself. It may be that you are happy with your physical appearance, but you keep attracting the wrong kind of relationships. Why? If we break our leg and don't go for treatment, we may never be able to walk again. It's the same with our mental health. If neglected, the damage can be for life. Counselling and behaviour therapies are free through the National Health Service (NHS) in the United Kingdom (UK); in the United States, insurance companies or health community programs may cover or discount the costs of such services as well. "Do you have unresolved injuries from the past that need some attention?"

Remember, this is all to be the best you possible. The foundation of any relationship starts with you. If your foundation is not stable, how can you expect to build on it?

I am passionate about this. Imagine yourself as a blank canvas: If there are splashes of paint all over the canvas, how can you have a fresh start? Prepare your canvas before you enter into any new relationship. Take the time to wipe it clean. Work through your own issues; have time out with just you. I know this sounds cliché, but people have told me "take time out to find out who you are." I used to think, *I don't want any more time on my own,* but I understand now how right they were. Imagine painting a room that has damp walls. As a quick fix, you paint over it. The dampness is still there; you've just done a great job of hiding it. Eventually it will come back through—the problem is still there. Sometimes jumping straight into a new relationship is just that way: you still have the same problems, which need to be addressed before any new relationship will work.

Here is a good example of how investing in yourself can change your life. My friend was dating a married man. In her eyes, everything was going great between them—until he left to go on a two-week holiday with his family. The two weeks that he was away made her realise that she wasn't his priority; he was never going to leave his situation. He was thousands of miles away, lying in the sun and working on his tan, while she was spending nights alone with only display cushions for company. They had been seeing each other for six months, and she was hooked. He was emotionally unavailable, but the more he made excuses, the more she craved his attention. The pattern of choosing emotionally unavailable men had become a lifestyle to my friend. The drama, the tears, and the anxiety had become addictive. Even though she didn't realise it, subconsciously, she enjoyed being let down. The relationship before that one had been a triangle where another woman was involved. If she wasn't falling for a man in a relationship, she was falling for a man who would never commit to her for other reasons.

My friend eventually went for counselling and behaviour therapy. During her sessions, it transpired that her father was a serial cheater, he had always had affairs, and her mother was always the victim. This had been all that she had seen throughout her childhood. Her mother wasn't very glamorous, but the women that her father had had affairs with were. This pattern of a three way relationship had become her life. My friend didn't know any other way as she had only seen that dynamic with her parents. She dressed very sexy, which was a result of the women she had seen with her father. She had received the message as a young child that looking sexy was how to get a man's attention, and she had learned that from the most important role model in her life. Men saw her as the good-time girl, and that impacted the lifespan of her relationships—they were always short-lived. Anyone who was emotionally available didn't interest her in the slightest; the emotionally unavailable man made her feel at home. It was all she had ever known.

After some cognitive behaviour therapy, my friend got to the root of the matter. When she made the connection and understood her own behaviour, it was life changing. She had invested in herself, and now she had a blank canvas and was ready to paint something magnificent. Now she had a solid foundation on which to build strong connections and relationships.

A male friend of mine is another example of investing in yourself. His relationships always followed the same pattern: he would meet a woman, fall in love, and then become possessive and needy. This resulted in his partners feeling smothered and then ending the relationship. He eventually hit rock bottom, and we discussed the possibility of him going for some counselling. Throughout the sessions it transpired that his mother had left the family for another man when my friend was young. His mother left the family home and never returned. He was left with his dad to bring him up, and he had very limited contact with his mother. The reason for his behaviour stemmed from his mother leaving. He had felt abandoned. He feared his relationships would end in a similar way, so he became needy and possessive. He feared losing those he loved, which had the opposite effect and pushed them away, resulting in a self-fulfilling prophecy. What he feared, he attracted, and it manifested itself within his own relationships. Making this connection and understanding his own behaviour helped him attract healthier partners and recognise when and why he was feeling insecure.

Another example I will share with you is about a woman who had a very dysfunctional childhood. Her adult relationships were short-lived, and she would often end her them before they got too serious. To the outside world she was a player, a woman who never wanted commitment. She came across as cold and emotionally detached. With some therapy, she explored her childhood. Her parents hadn't been there for her or her siblings while growing up. As the eldest, she would often have to take responsibility for her siblings. Her parents worked long hours and were rarely at home at meal times. There was no affection or love shown by either parent. This impacted on her adult relationships. She would struggle to show affection because she didn't really know how too. She would often sabotage her relationships if she felt partners were getting too close. Her partners would often describe her as cold, but that wasn't the case—she just didn't know how to express her feelings. Her parents had led separate lives; they never did anything as a couple, and their example manifested itself in her relationships.

Each member of a family, even when brought up in the same house, will be affected in different ways by what he or she experiences. There is always a reason for a certain behaviour. It is just about taking the time to explore and understand why. If we understand why we feel and behave in a certain way, it can be life changing.

Another story I will share is about a woman who was always involved with possessive men. The men she dated were controlling and she always followed the same pattern, her relationships were destructive and unhealthy.

Looking back into her childhood her father was a big drinker, he was very controlling with her mother. It wasn't unusual for her to be kept awake at night with her parents arguing. Although her mother did try to be there for her, neither parent met her emotional needs.

The reason she gravitated towards possessive men was because it made her feel loved and wanted. Something she craved, the attention she received from the drama and the controlling behaviour made her feel wanted. As outsiders, we can often judge and make assumptions about people, but when we peel back the layers there is always a reason. The power is understanding why, so we can make the connection and start attracting healthier relationships.

Before you consider new relationships or dates, start with a clean canvas. This is doubly important for people who have come out of long-term relationships. Give yourself time to heal and grieve—again, a cliché, but so valuable and so true.

The best dating advice I could give you, is before you start to get to know someone new, get to know yourself. Knowing yourself is like navigating around an iceberg; you can see your problems and challenges before you hit them. Knowing why you are attracted to certain people is powerful and the key ingredient to all relationships.

OBSERVE WHAT YOU ATTRACT

I once had a conversation with a high-powered businessman who made huge decisions regarding global companies. He spoke to me about his ex-wife. He also described how he had suffered for many years while married, as his wife had been difficult and had suffered from mental-health problems.

The question most people don't ask themselves is "Why am I attracting this person?" or "Why is she [or he] attracted to me?"

It is true: birds of a feather flock together. This may be in the form of a victim and a rescuer, but never make the mistake of judging others without asking those same questions yourself. If you are attracting the same men or women over and over and repeating the same patterns, dig deep and ask yourself, "What kind of childhood did I have? Am I attracted to unhealthy situations?" The answers will be there; they lay in your past. You can change the pattern. The first step is recognising it and then getting help to change it, as with the case studies I shared earlier. It is easy to blame others but much harder to hold a mirror up to ourselves. Taking responsibility and recognising our own behaviour is the key.

I spoke earlier about cleaning your canvas: Imagine the different colours a painter uses to create a picture. The primary colours are red, yellow, and blue, and other colours can be made from them. For example, if you mix blue and yellow together you can make green. But some combinations are not complementary. It's like that with people. If you mix certain people together, it can be a recipe for disaster; they can bring out each other's demons, in essence, their true colors or their worst colours. It is important to get help and deal with our own issues, but it is also important to understand that mixing two types of people together can sometimes be magical, but it also can be unhealthy. Take ownership for your stuff, and remember to look at how your behaviour may contribute to someone else's.

THE EMPTY BASKET CONCEPT

If you only have one egg in the dating game, what are you left with once it's gone? An empty basket. The egg you have appears more desirable because it is the only egg you have. You have everything riding on that one egg. Have lots of eggs in your basket, and you will appear more desirable.

An example of this comes from a friend of mine. She had arranged a date with a guy and invested hours of texting and getting to know him, neglecting all other suitors. Then, one day before the date, he cancelled. She was deeply affected by this and responded from an emotional place, which made her look completely irrational. As you can probably guess, there was no date.

Let's imagine she had lots of suitors and didn't engage too much prior to this one date. If he had let her down, would she have responded in the same way? Most likely not.

Always have lots of eggs in your basket, and by eggs I mean options. Having more options allow us to appear and to feel less desperate. If a guy cancels, it's not the end of the world—no empty basket. These options don't have to be men; they can be spending time with friends or with family. Just feel that you have alternatives.

Never respond from an emotional place. Some guys will play it cool or will cancel just to see how you will react. Always react with dignity and grace. These people are not the be all and end all. Be cool, and if a guy is messing you around, make a dignified exit, and let him move on to the next person.

Someone close to me went through a similar scenario. Since she was new to the dating world, I offered her some of my advice. However, sometimes people have to learn from their own mistakes.

My friend had recently separated from her husband, and she decided to try online dating. She met a guy who lived a good five hours away from her. They spent hours every day calling and texting each other. Ultimately, she was convinced she had met "the one." I told her to wait until she met him in person before she invested more of her emotions. It really is true; until you have met someone in person, you don't know how you're going to feel.

The night arrived when my friend was to meet her date. He had booked a hotel, and they both agreed that since he had to travel so far, he would stay the whole weekend. They arranged to have a few drinks near his hotel. I told her to keep in touch and let me know how it was going. The hours went by and no text; I assumed she must have liked him and all was going well.

Later that evening, I received a phone call. My friend was disappointed and completely disheartened. He didn't look at all like his photographs, and she just didn't fancy him. Since he had traveled so far, she had felt obligated to stay and entertain him—even though all she wanted to do was leave. My friend felt guilty because he had paid to stay the whole weekend, but she just couldn't face spending any more time with him when she knew it wasn't going to work out. After the awkward evening, she left. There was no further contact between them.

My friend learned a valuable lesson that day. She had put all her energy into that one egg, so when it didn't work out, she felt empty and back to square one, having to start all over again. If she had had a few eggs in her basket, she wouldn't have felt so disappointed. She would have had other distractions to focus on rather than dwelling on her wasted time.

The whole situation was hard for her to accept because she felt that she had something special with him, but you can form a connection with many people, especially if you enjoy the same hobbies and hold many of the same values. However, what distinguishes a friend from a partner is the physical chemistry and spark that everybody longs for.

This brings up the subject of online dating. Of course, it provides many great benefits, and there are many success stories. However, you have to be vigilant when you are looking for a partner. Have you ever bought a dress online, and when it arrived you felt it looked nothing like the photo? You instantly didn't like it and could tell immediately that it wouldn't look right on you, so you sent it back. The same disappointment can happen with online dating. When you meet the person, he may not be at all as you imagined.

Another thing to take into consideration is distance. If you don't mind distance, that's okay, but you still should be realistic. You can get so carried away with trying to find the right guy that you forget to read the small print. Don't just look at the pictures. Distance, as we saw in the last scenario, can create problems. The guy had committed to a whole weekend with my friend, spending money and time traveling, only to return home disappointed.

Bad experiences can put people off online dating, which is why I think it is important to highlight things that you can do—and signs you can watch for—to create a positive experience. In the back of this book, I have compiled some guidelines that will help you avoid situations like the above scenario.

The key point of this concept is keep your options open, don't close the lid on your basket when it only has one egg in. There will come a time when you will want to do that, however in the initial stages of dating, have lots of eggs in your basket.

LIVING IN REVERSE

After a disappointing date, it is easy to slip into negative thinking, questioning whether there is anyone out there for you. It can sometimes throw you back into the arms of an ex-boyfriend, someone you know and feel comfortable with. But remember Frankenstein's concept: it is over for a reason, so don't take the easy option, which will most likely never work. The truth is, you will probably have many bad dates, but it is all good fun and definitely something to cheer up your friends with when you share your stories.

You have to keep going. Who knows? That next date might just be the one. It will happen; you just have to have faith. We have two choices: move forward or move backward. If you go back to what you know, you're reversing. Do you want to live every day as you did yesterday? I call this living in reverse. Would you like to live your life in reverse? Or do you want to move forward? Hold onto that thought.

A classic example of living in reverse is going back to an ex after a bad date. You go back and feel great for a few weeks. Your life seems back to normal, and you feel human again. Then the arguments start, and you wonder why you went back in the first place. Where might you be if you had stayed strong? You know, deep down, that going back wasn't the right thing. It's hard being on your own—it seems so much easier standing together as a couple. However, if you know a relationship is not right, you are simply prolonging the pain. It's like missing your exit. You now have to drive to the next junction to get back on the same route. Know when it's time to take the exit. It is your time you're wasting.

The next time you feel the need to go back to an ex-boyfriend for the wrong reasons, think about this concept.

HAVE A DESTINATION

You don't get on a train and let it take you just anywhere. You have a destination. So why sit in the passenger seat of your own train? Get in the driver's seat; have a plan.

The first step to any goal is a destination. What do you want? Where do you want to be?

Try to figure out what it is you are looking for in a partner. Stability? Romance? Just a friendship? When you decide what you want, make a plan to get it.

The reason why I think this is valuable to share is because of my own experience. I once started dating someone who wanted to start a family, and, at the time, I didn't. I ignored it in the beginning, purely because I liked him so much. I kidded myself that his priorities and wishes would change to suit mine, and I hoped we would figure it out. I have a grown son, and so I knew I didn't want to have any more children. Even though I had made myself clear in the beginning, he was hoping that I would change my mind. We spent six months together, and the relationship was going great until the subject of children cropped up again. I wasn't willing to compromise, nor was he. Even though we worked well together in every other aspect of the relationship, it just couldn't continue because we both saw our futures differently.

I had a destination. I knew where I wanted to be, and so did he. We had both wasted valuable time together that could have been spent with people who had the same wants and goals. This was a clear example of not reading the road signs. Looking back, it was right there in front of me. The route was mapped out, and there was a roadblock at the end, but I still went down the road. When I got there, there was no other option but to turn around. I was back to square one.

I learned a great lesson from this, and from that day on, I was meticulous about what I wanted and made it clear from the beginning. You have got to be honest with yourself and recognise when a relationship is worthy of your time and has longevity.

If you don't have a goal or destination, where are you going? The message is this: know what you want and where you want to be.

"Don't look for bread in the meat aisle"

DON'T LOOK FOR BREAD IN THE MEAT AISLE

When you are wandering around the supermarket looking for, let's say, bread, you don't go to the meat aisle to look for it. If you ask for a type of bread in the meat aisle, they will look at you like you're stupid. You know exactly where to find bread.

It's the same thing in the dating world. If you want a specific type of guy, where will you find him? If you want a suit guy who drinks champagne and enjoys the high life, where is he most likely to be? Do your research the same way you would if you were looking for a job. If you prefer the musician type, where is he most likely to hang out? Get yourself to some concerts and gigs. Mr. Right is not going to knock on your door. Create your own "being in the right place at the right time."

A classic example of this comes from a friend. She was obsessed with rugby players; she loved the sport and loved the game. At every opportunity, she would go to watch rugby. Afterward, she would socialise where they would hang out. My friend has only ever dated sports men. Through her genuine interest, she has met the kind of man she likes. My friend placed herself in the right place at the right time—it really is that simple.

If you are looking for a certain type of dress, you go to a certain type of shop. Common sense, wouldn't you say? Apply that principle to the partner you are hoping to attract.

HELPFUL GUIDELINES

Are you considering online dating? When choosing dating sites, think carefully before you jump in. I would opt for sites where you have to pay, as people there are more likely to be looking for a relationship. Think about what type of people go on each different site. Do your research. Talk to friends who have been on dating sites. Read reviews. Do your homework.

Number One

Be wary of individuals who have photos that are just headshots. My first online date was a disaster! He had only posted headshots, but being new to the dating world, I didn't even consider that he wouldn't look like his pictures. The evening of the date came, and I was shocked. I'm convinced that the pictures he'd posted were of his brother! I'm just being honest. He was a very large man, and I just wasn't attracted to him. I felt cheated, as he hadn't posted appropriate pictures of himself. I spent the night counting the minutes until I could escape.

I shared a story earlier where my friend had the same experience. Read the small print. Some women prefer a larger man; it's not something I find myself attracted to. If there is only one picture and you aren't sure, ask for more pictures—in the most polite way possible, of course. For example, "You look great! It would lovely to see a few more pictures of you."

This works both ways; I understand we want to look our best and post our favourite photographs, but make sure you post up to date pictures.

If they're expecting to meet you as you were ten years ago, you're setting yourself up for failure. Just think about how you would feel if you were on the receiving end. Embrace who you are and be true to yourself.

Number Two

Always make the first date a quick coffee or drink where you limit yourself to an hour. If he's not for you, it's easier to escape without hurting anyone's feelings. If you think he is great, that's great! You can stay longer or arrange another date. I would also recommend a quick phone call prior to meeting. You may learn that you have no spark over the phone and then you're not wasting your time by meeting. I have had conversations with guys over the phone and really struggled; it can be a great way of finding out if you will get along.

Number Three

Avoid long-term texting with an online connection who you haven't met in person. It's distracting. You will not know if you like someone until you actually meet him or her. There is no point investing hours of your time texting and calling, only to meet and discover that there is no physical attraction. It's disappointing. I made this mistake and invested hours with someone over the phone. As soon as we met in person, game over—no chemistry. I was so disappointed. One phone call is all that is necessary. Some people prefer to meet in person rather than speak over the phone. Do whatever works best for you.

Number Four

We all have a framework for how we respond and react to things. For example, two people see the same fight and yet interpret it differently. One may see one person as the victim; one may see that same person as the aggressor. This assumption is drawn from our own personal experiences. Texting in the dating game can be fun, but it also can be difficult. We don't know the tone or the humour a text is sent with unless we really know the person. I have seen many women read a text and take it the wrong way or get the wrong impression. Communication is the key. Keep texting simple: send "How's your day?" rather than typing out long, meaningful conversations.

Number Five

What should you wear? This is an important one, as you want him to see *you*, not just your sexiness. I have made the mistake of wearing outfits that were too sexy, and it has sent out the wrong message. Dates have taken one look at me and, because I have a nice figure and wear sexy clothes, they have assumed that I am not intelligent or not girlfriend material. Ridiculous, I know; however, men are wired a certain way. If you show up with six-inch heels and a revealing outfit, what first impression do you think he is getting? In time, you can pull out the sexy outfits—because you are who you are!—but the spark needs to come from a connection, a mental connection not just a physical one.

Most relationships that come purely from a physical place don't last. For example, I have been in a roomful of men when an overtly sexy women walks in wearing a short skirt and high heels. Yes, she gets the men's attention, but when she has left the room they will make comments like "I wouldn't kick her out of bed." On the other hand, I have been sitting in a roomful of men when a woman has walked in who was not so overtly sexy, wearing a more understated outfit, and when she has left the room they have related to her in a different way, saying things like "She's girlfriend material." I am not saying that wearing short skirts is a problem; I love sexy clothes. However, in the world of dating, you want a man's attention that will last a lifetime, not just five minutes. There is nothing sexier than a woman who is comfortable in her own skin.

Some women feel they should dress up, and some women feel that they're most sexy in a jeans and T-shirt. Wear what makes you feel confident, but remember what message you are sending. First impressions are powerful.

Number Six

Never sleep with a man straight away, no matter how much you like him. It is advice as old as time—and for a reason! I have witnessed men go crazy over women in the initial stages, but I have also seen them lose interest overnight when they sleep with someone too soon.

I worked with a guy who was really into this girl. They would text all day long. He seemed really into her, but on the first official date, they slept together. I saw his attitude change overnight!

Women can make the mistake of thinking that sex will make a man more interested. That is so wrong! For the decent guys out there, it has the reverse effect. Sex after a buildup of dates is a different story. Men want a challenge; they want you to make them wait. Men like the chase. Some men need to feel you are hard to attain, and they will go to great lengths if they want to see you again. Make them work for your time. In fact, make it impossible to see you all the time. If they want you, they will make an effort.

A true life example of this comes from a relative of mine. A guy she knew through work had pursued her persistently for a number of months, when she finally agreed to go on a date with him, one thing led to another and they ended up sleeping together. After that night, he never contacted her again. Had she waited longer, the outcome may have been different. He told one of her colleagues that he was attracted to her because she was a challenge, however he lost interest because she gave in too soon, and in his eyes he had conquered her too quickly.

Don't put yourself in a position where sex might happen in the very early stages. No sleeping over at his place after the first date. Let him wine and dine you. Spend time getting to know one another. As soon as a woman has sex, the dynamics change. For her, it becomes a relationship, but for a guy, if it's only been two minutes and you are jumping into bed with him, he will look at you more as a good-time girl than a woman he will see a future with. Every single man I have spoken to and observed has confirmed it: a man sees a woman differently if she makes him wait.

Number Seven

It is very important when going on dates to let someone know where you are. Never arrange dates at your home address. Do not arrange to be collected from there either. Give out as limited personal data as possible until you are completely comfortable with that person. Safeguarding yourself is paramount. I am aware of circumstances where women have been asked for large amounts of money from individuals they have met on-line. After establishing an emotional connection, they have shared a personal crisis which is followed by a request for money. Although it seems common sense not to send money to someone you have never met, some men and women who are vulnerable can be too trusting.

My friend's mother was a victim of online fraud. She joined an on-line dating site after being single for a number of years. She described falling in love with a man on-line, even though they had never met. It may seem hard to conceive, however strong connections can be formed without actually meeting a person. After they had been in communication for a number of weeks, he had asked for a large amount of money for his son whom he maintained was extremely ill. She agreed to send the money to him but once the money had been received, contact from him stopped and his profile disappeared.

This is just one example of many. Cyber-crime is on the increase, there are professional criminals online who will actively seek out dating sites solely for this purpose.

These scenarios can be avoided. Always ask for a second opinion if you're not sure about a person or situation. On-line dating can be lots of fun and is a great way of meeting new people but remain vigilant.

GET THE RIGHT EXPOSURE

This leads nicely to getting the right exposure. If all you do is drive to work and back, and have the occasional trip to visit your friends, how are you going to meet someone?

Life is all about getting the right exposure. A classic example of this is my sister and I. As children, we shared bunk beds. We were both brought up in the same family home. I work a seventy-hour week, and she flies around the world first class and has houses all over; she is living the dream. You might ask why. Is it destiny? Is it fate? I do believe in fate, but why not put yourself in the right place at the right time?

My sister worked hard and got a job working for a huge global company. Successful in her own right, she was exposed to rich, powerful men—the type of men I wouldn't be exposed to. The result? I work hard to have one holiday a year, and she flies around the world first class, married to her dream guy. Are we not here to live the best life possible? I know that people say money isn't everything, but it sure does help. How about your dream guy who is solvent and successful? Do your research. If you want a certain kind of man, where will you find him? You may never have a job where you will meet him, but you can socialise in places that he might. You can go on holiday where he might. Take up a new sport or hobby—say tennis or squash—which offer great places to meet eligible men.

A fantastic example of this comes from a friend of mine. She became single after her relationship had broken down. My friend didn't like the idea of dating sites, and so she joined a tennis club. She had always wanted to play tennis, and now, with time on her hands, she finally decided to take the plunge. This changed my friend's life. Not only did she meet a very eligible single guy, but it opened so many other doors—she was invited to all sorts of events. That one change had a huge impact on her life.

When I decided to write this book, I started looking online for book events. I signed up for a three-day conference to help me achieve my goal. That weekend was amazing. I met so many incredible, like-minded people, and we shared a common goal: we all wanted to write a book. We formed a social group, and each day everyone would share quotes and stories that motivated us all. I didn't find romance, but I found friends, information, and inspiration, which are priceless. Remember, meeting just one new person can open many new doors.

NEVER CONFORM

I went on holiday for a week with a large group of people for a special event. That trip opened my eyes to society and how some people see single people. I noticed that there was a clique at meal times—couples. I felt like I had two heads because I was single. The usual comment, "Are you still single?" was said in a way that seemed to be almost a crime. It did bother me, and I found myself quietly slipping out early on a few occasions. If I could go back to that time I would never have allowed anyone to make me feel inadequate because I was single. Let me let you in on a secret: I have heard numerous stories of how both men and women are bored and unhappy, have no sex life, and long for more than what their current relationship has to offer. Don't be that girl who conforms, who settles down with the first guy who comes along so that you can fit in with your friends. Be that girl who is confident to be standing alone at the party, because in my experience, many married people are married because of the kids, because they are scared of being alone, or because of financial reasons and family pressure. Get it right. There are so many positives to being single and knowing you can be alone because you choose to be, not because you're terrified of being on your own. Be that person who waited for the right guy and who is now happily married.

A classic example of acting on social pressure to be in a relationship is the next story I will share with you.

This woman craved marriage. All of her friends were getting married and having children. This put pressure on her, and she would berate herself as to why she hadn't met anyone yet. She always made references about time running out. This affected her so much that she admitted to me that she knew the man she was marrying might not be the right guy. She was settling down because he was first guy who came along. She admitted that he was not the right guy. This woman craved so much to be someone's wife and fit in with her social group that she was prepared to ignore her feelings and marry someone who was not right for her. I remember having a conversation with her at another friend's wedding, which I knew was a difficult day for her as it appeared that everyone's life was moving forward—except for hers. I told her that it wasn't her time yet, and when her time did come, it would be worth waiting for.

But she wasn't convinced, and, after three years, she finally got her fairy-tale wedding. The following year she had a child. She was now someone's wife. However, it didn't feel at all like she thought it would. She was unhappier than she ever had been. Her self-esteem suffered a great deal, and she lost all confidence in herself. After childbirth, her body changed, and instead of being happy in the relationship and focusing on the new chapter in her life, her partner didn't give her the support to embrace her new body and help her get back to the weight she was happy with. This was all magnified because she was with the wrong person. She spent most of her nights in, while he was out with his friends. The marriage lasted less than two years, and now she is divorced and bringing up a child as a single parent. Had she not felt so strongly about conforming, she might never have been in that position. Of course, she got a beautiful child out of it, but if she could go back, she openly admits that she would have done things differently.

So, next time you get the patronising question, "Are you still single?" remember that story. Be patient, and make sure you wait for the right guy. It will be worth it in the long run.

No pain, no gain!

ARE YOU CHOOSING BETWEEN TWO GUYS?

Have you ever listened to a girlfriend who likes two guys and spends hours mulling over which guy she prefers? If you're choosing between two guys and you don't know which one to choose, more often than not, neither will be right for you. Let me tell you, when you know, you know. It's like trying on a dress. You know instantly if you like it and if you're going to buy it. The one you hemmed and hawed about whether to buy, either never gets worn or gets returned. Men aren't as easy to return if you decide they aren't for you; you should know which one without question, without hesitation. Both might be great guys, but, if you're even contemplating choosing, I would question whether either are right for you. There are some cases where in the beginning people have a choice and it works out however, my point is would you be happy if you learned your partner was contemplating between you and another woman? Food for thought.

DON'T BUY A HOUSE WITHOUT VIEWING IT

Okay, you're looking around for your dream home. You have the money; you just need to find the right one. You look online and see an amazing house. It seems to tick all your boxes. Do you buy it without at least a few viewings? Of course you don't. You might go inside and find out that the bathroom is not up to your standards or the living area is too small. So why do we rush into relationships? Should we commit to a life with someone after a short period of time? Make sure you take a good look around in all the rooms before you commit to forever after. Would we buy the first house that came along, or would we see what's out there, waiting awhile?

This takes us back to never having an empty basket. Create options so that you can be satisfied that you're not buying because you think it's all that's available. Buy when it's what you really want and, more importantly, when you have waited to see the surveyor's report or appraisal!

A true example of this comes from one of my close friends who met a guy. She was vulnerable at the time and had low self-esteem. She had just come out of a difficult relationship. Within six months she was engaged. Both were professionals. In the beginning, he was attentive. He spent time with her son and came across as the perfect partner. As time elapsed, the surveyor's report came back. It transpired that he was in debt, and he had to pay hundreds of pounds out of his wage a month. He had one daughter who he barely saw, and his true colours with her son came to light. He would sit upstairs while her son sat downstairs, and he made it known that he didn't have much time for him.

Further, my friend learned that he suffered from depression. Funnily enough, he was the life and soul of the party. He had a picture of his daughter on his desk at work, also portraying a different persona. After five years of struggle—and when he had paid the debt off—he left my friend on New Year's Day. Inconsolable and crushed and approaching fifty, she felt that she would never recover and now admits she stayed with him out of the fear that she wouldn't find anyone else at her age. The good news is that it's now one year later, and she's never been happier. I had signed her up with an online dating service, took a few nice pictures for her, and she is now dating and loving life. Her ex also joined a dating site, and he met a wealthy woman; the same cycle began again within a short period of time, and he proposed. She has posted pictures of him playing with her children, portraying the perfect father figure. We know the reality.

Let's rewind.

Pied Piper Concept- I will talk about this concept in a later chapter. Had he told her what she wanted to hear? Of course, he did. She was so focused on having someone in her life she went along with everything he said without question.

Road signs—were there any? Maybe not straight away, but look at someone's past, look at their relationships with their family, children, and friends. That will tell you so much about a person. Remember, actions speak louder than words. Why had his previous relationship broken down? Why didn't he see his daughter very much? Why was he in debt? Why didn't he have a house by the time he was in his forties? Why did he want to rush into marriage? These were all road signs that my friend chose to ignore. Did that choice cost her five years on the motorway? Yes.

I shared this story not to scare you but to raise awareness. Because only when the roof is caving in on the house we bought without waiting for the surveyor's report do we start reading the small print. I want women to stick together. My heart goes out to the new girlfriend, but if my friend had tried to warn her, how would she have been received? Not very well. By not rushing in, we can save ourselves from a roof falling down. Let's say that he turned out to be everything that she ever dreamed of. Would it be so hard to wait? We should always take our time before laying down big deposits—before we invest our lives in people and in any third-party children.

A person may project a certain image, just as a house may appear warm and cozy, but the report may show damp in the walls or woodworm in the loft. Don't rush in.

If you settle for someone for the wrong reasons—for example, so that you are not alone—time passes and you start making commitments. Then what happens if you suddenly meet your dream guy? It's like rushing into buying a house and compromising your wants for the sake of just buying something. Six months later, a house comes up with more bedrooms for less money in the key location you had wanted. The problem is that you have already committed to something you didn't really want. The message here is take your time. Be sure you are 100 percent certain you have made the right decision (and for the right reasons) before you make huge commitments.

ALWAYS GO WITH YOUR INSTINCT

The most powerful tool we have as human beings is instinct. When you don't know what to do or which path to take, your instinct will know. When your head hits the pillow at night and you toss and turn, it is your gut talking. When you're driving and thoughts come into your mind that something isn't just right, trust them. Human beings are fascinating creations; just as our bodies tell us when we are hungry or ill, they also communicate on a deeper level. What is your gut saying to you?

If you have a feeling that your partner is cheating, eight times out of ten you will be right. Intuition is a powerful tool. However, let's not get confused with being paranoid. It's important to give trust to others until they give us a reason not to.

Your gut feeling is the one in the pit of your stomach. It's not something you rationalise with; it's the first thing that comes into your mind when you let your guard down with yourself and ask yourself difficult questions.

Think about the times when you've had a gut feeling about someone or something. I am confident that most people are right about a situation when that happens. Use that internal tool—it's free and can be a great friend when you need one.

If someone throws a ball at your face, what does your instinct do? It reacts. It responds immediately without thinking it through or waiting a few seconds for the ball to hit your face.

Our emotional instinct is the same as our physical instinct. It is there to protect us. We all have that instinct—so use it.

ACTIONS SPEAK LOUDER THAN WORDS

When I have a question about someone's behaviour, I don't look at what they say—I look at what they do. Anyone can use words, but people's actions tell us the real story. For example, just look at your friends, the ones who are really there for you, not the ones who are only there when it's all fun and games. Look at the man you're dating. Is he making an effort? Is he pulling out all the stops? Or is it all false promises? The next time you are wondering about something, use this concept and look at people's actions.

An example of this comes from a friend of mine. Her partner had had a brief affair, however, they had worked through it and had gotten back together. I listened to her telling me that things were great, but her actions told a different story. Although she maintained that she was happy, she was still checking his phone on a regular basis. Prior to the infidelity, she was always the life and soul of the party, whereas now she always seemed withdrawn and not herself. Due to the change in her behaviour I asked how things were at home, it transpired that her partner was still in contact with the other woman. Every time she questioned him about the contact, he would come up with an excuse.

Let's look at his actions. They tell us everything we need to know. If he valued the relationship, he wouldn't keep in contact with the other woman. If he really wanted to rebuild trust, was that the way to do it?

In relationships, people will often say they love you, but do you feel loved? Do you ever find yourself asking someone if they love you, hoping for some sort of validation? People can say many things, but when you need really need them, what are their actions saying? Do the words match the picture?

Actions speak louder than words. This concept can be used in every aspect of your life. When in doubt, look at people's actions.

BE A FRIEND TO YOURSELF

It's a famous saying: be a friend to yourself. It seems to be common sense, doesn't it? So why aren't we a friend to ourselves? Why do we do things that we don't want to do? Why do we date guys who bring us nothing but drama or anxiety? It's something to think about. The next time you think about doing something that you know isn't right or good for you, ask yourself, "Am I being a friend to myself?"

I like to turn things around: what I would tell a good friend to do if she was in my position? That always helps put situations in the right perspective.

We are all good at dishing out advice. So the next time you are in a situation that warrants advice from your friends, ask yourself one question first: what would I tell myself?

BE A FRIEND TO OTHERS

I know how hard life can sometimes seem as a single woman. When your friends are married or have partners, it's really difficult to find people to go out with. I think that women need to be reminded of this: If or when things go wrong, you will still need your friends. If you make your partner your entire life, you will have no balance.

I have found myself not being invited to social events because they were all couples, and some of the women didn't want single women hanging around because they were insecure. When you are happy and are dating, look out for your single friends—they need your support. Many of my single friends have experienced feeling isolated from social events. This can be one of the most difficult things about being single. The key is to take up a new hobby; join a running group or walking group. It's amazing how many people are out there in the same boat. Remember, get the right exposure!

THE SUPPLY TEACHER

Can you remember being in high school when they brought in a supply teacher? It was an hour of flying paper airplanes and catching up with your friends. Some women become a supply teacher with men; they allow men to walk all over them.

Don't be a supply teacher. Have boundaries that encourage respect. Does he text you a few hours before asking to meet, expecting you to be free? Does he mess you around? Does he let you down but expect that things will be okay after one "I'm sorry" text? Supply teacher, you know who you are!

My friend was classic supply teacher. She was doing all the chasing, asking this guy to meet up all the time. The more he rejected her and the longer he took to reply, the more it made her want him. My friend justified chasing him by saying that if she didn't contact him, he wouldn't contact her, and she really liked him.

You can be wearing the classiest clothes and have the most beautiful face, but real class is having self-esteem and self-respect. That's sexier than a pair of high heels and a stunning dress. Think back to the men you knew you could walk all over. Did you have passion for them? Did you count the hours until you received your next text? I think the answer will be no. It works both ways. If he won't meet you halfway, he's not worth meeting at all. Next!

Relationships shouldn't be hard work. With my friend, an intervention was required. First, I told her to slap herself—hard! I made her go cold turkey and not contact him. He was used to the attention daily and would miss it. He had never texted her first because he knew he didn't have to. My friend would text him and not get a reply for hours. It would consume her: she wouldn't be present in the moment, constantly looking at her phone and obsessing as to why he hadn't replied. The result was that every rejection, every "I'm too busy to meet up," every missing reply was knocking her confidence. Yes, she would feel good for a few seconds when he finally replied, but afterward she would feel bad for having to do all the chasing.

Think of drug users who really need a hit. Once they have it, it's great for a short while. Then they come down. Every time it gets worse, and they become more and more dependent and addicted.

It's the same with our behaviour. Cold turkey is damn hard but worth it. My friend went a week with no reply. He knew from her past behaviour that she would more than likely break; he had her down as the supply teacher. Eventually he broke. That's called meeting you halfway.

The key here is that the right guy will do more than meet you halfway—he will do 110 percent. Their relationship was an unhealthy dynamic from the start. The only reason I advised my friend to do the above was to regain her self-esteem, but that guy was not Mr. Right, and she knew it.

Look at your own relationships. Are you a supply teacher?

THE PIED PIPER

I think children's stories have a lot of strong messages. One of the stories is that of the pied piper: he plays lovely music in order to get the rats to follow him. They are all hypnotised by the music and follow without question. The destination? A room that is filled with rats! I use this example to show how we listen to what we want to hear and tune out the rest. And then, when things go wrong and we end up in a roomful of rats, we ask ourselves, "How did I get here? How did I get sucked in again?"

A friend of mine did this exact thing. She dated a guy who, in the beginning, appeared together and solvent. He ran his own business, showed up in the flash car, and was attentive—what a catch! As time went on, he proposed in Paris, and she was delighted and accepted. From that day forth, things deteriorated. As soon as he had that commitment and that ring on her finger, the cracks started to show: It transpired that he did not own the car; it was on a personal contract purchase (PCP). The business he ran was in debt. He drank most nights, which became a problem. And, soon after their marriage, she found out that he was on medication for depression. My friend spent most of her weekends alone while her husband was out on his motorbike, and she often opted for early nights while he stayed up and drank red wine.

Tied to him financially and emotionally, at thirty-one years old she was worrying about her future. She had nothing to call her own, and she still wanted a family. But if she left, where would she go? What would she do? How would she face her friends who had paid large sums to fly out to her dream wedding?

Let's rewind.

Always read the road signs. Could she have seen this coming? Did she read the signs?

Did she have plenty of viewings before she purchased the house? No, she rushed in without shopping around.

She didn't wait for the surveyor's report. By the time it came in, all her time and money were invested.

The pied piper concept was in play here. She saw what she wanted to see. She ignored the signs. She was so desperate for the dream wedding and dream guy that she went along with it. She was hypnotised—focused on being someone's wife, on fitting in with all her friends, and on not being alone. And what about the destination? Was it to her liking? No, it was "How did I get here?"

Did she want to conform? Did she feel social pressure because all of her friends were married with children? Yes, she did.

The result was wasted years of her life—being with the wrong person instead of waiting for the right person. In the end, people were judging her because her marriage didn't last.

CLIMB THE HILL OR TAKE THE FLAT ROUTE?

I was out walking with my friends. By my own admission, I was not as fit as they were. We stood at a crossroads: the options were a steep hill, which was almost vertical, or a nice flat landscape. I wanted to walk the flat as I wanted a nice easy walk. I was outvoted, and we took the hill. My face was red. I was uncomfortable and felt very unfit. At the top, I caught my breath and took in the view. It was magnificent! I looked at how far we had come, and I was so glad that I had been talked into taking the hill. I wouldn't have seen the beautiful view had we opted for the easier route.

I tell that story because it's like being single. It is so hard to admit that the guy wasn't for you or that it didn't work out. It's hard to say that, yes, he was nice, and he would have been great company, but you just weren't feeling it. It's hard to say, yes, another date just didn't work out. You begin to ask yourself, "Is it me? Am I too fussy?"

It's hard to tell a guy where to go if he's messing you around when you really like him. It may seem easier to put up with the issues and have the guy by your side.

What about the guy who is safe and is a nice guy but just not the right guy? Let me tell you, you will never have your breath taken away. If you want the magnificent, you have to be patient. You have to take chances and not buy the first house that comes up for sale. If you want to be treated amazingly, then you are going to have to opt for the hill and not the flat route. When you are standing at the top, you have the self-esteem to say, "Thanks, but you just aren't treating me like I expect or deserve to be treated." When you get to that place, which is a hard climb, you will look back and see how far you have come; you will like being on the top of the mountain.

An example of this happened to me with a guy I liked. We had met at mutual friends' parties a few times. It was clear that we both liked each other, but it took him a year and a half to get my number and ask me out. We agreed on a venue and set a date for Friday, which was five days away. I didn't text him, as I didn't want to appear too eager. By Thursday, I still hadn't heard from him, but I was hopeful that he would get in touch later that evening at the very latest. I had gotten a spray tan, dyed my hair, had my eyebrows plucked within an inch of their life, and spent the day trying on outfits. I was all set! Thursday evening came and still no contact. I drove home that evening very frustrated, but I wasn't going to chase him. If he wanted a date, he would have to chase me. Friday morning came and no messages. I was so disappointed (empty-basket concept). It got to be one in the afternoon, and I finally received a text from him—he was asking me if I was in town! I told him I thought it was incredibly rude to contact me an hour before we had arranged to meet, and I said that I was no longer interested.

I really wanted to see him, but I knew he didn't value the date. I felt it was rude and not gentlemanly. If I had met him that day or rearranged our date to suit him, he would have had no respect for me (supply teacher). I had to take the hill instead of the flat route.

TEACUP RIDE OR ROLLER COASTER?

This is one of my favourite concepts, and one that I truly believe in. We have all seen the teacup ride. It goes around and around, staying at the same speed. You know that it's safe and completely reliable. Then there is the roller coaster. There is always a massive line to board. Once you're on it and climbing to the top, you feel adrenaline begin to surge and wonder why you got on! When it starts its downward dive, you fly around with your head banging from side to side and feel sick. You're up, you're down, and, before you know it, you come to a halt with the wind still blowing through your hair and the blood still pounding in your veins. You vow you will never get on again—but you always do.

I think this is a lot like relationships. Those who opt for the teacup ride are safe and secure. They aren't going to fall off. There is no risk. It's completely reliable, however, after a few rides it becomes boring. Those on the teacup ride look over at the roller coaster and long to be there. It's the same with men. Women and men who settle for safety eventually get bored. There is no challenge, and that's when affairs can happen.

Then there is the roller coaster. Although I wouldn't recommend the roller coaster full time, I do recommend a few rides. The roller coaster gets your blood pumping—you feel sick; your head is spinning; and you feel your heart in your mouth. You feel totally alive for a few seconds.

You even check your seat belt to make sure you're strapped in. The worry! The adrenaline! It's great for a few rides, but eventually the roller coaster gets to be too much.

The roller coaster is similar to exciting but destructive relationships, the ones that are great when they are great but very bad when they are bad, the kind that are up and down and eventually can't be maintained.

The teacup ride refers to the relationships we find ourselves in that are safe and secure—but that's all. These relationships are the ones that are good on paper, but, deep down, you know you are settling for safety. These kinds of relationships are often where the partner feels like your best friend, but there is no spark. In this relationship, you feel you won't get hurt.

It's about finding a balance. If you settle for the teacup ride, you may have safety, but does it make you feel alive? If you are always on the roller coaster, it will end up taking its toll on your health. The key is finding a balance and not settling for second best or buying the first house that comes up for sale.

You didn't come all this way from the womb for a teacup ride, did you?

Are you dating a roller coaster? Or teacup ride?

"Are you dating a roller coaster?"

THE POWER OF NO REPLY

Let's look back into history at women who had a huge influence over men. My favourite, Anne Boleyn, made Henry VIII, the king of England, break with the Catholic Church. Why? It was because she was unattainable; she was strong and didn't give in like all the other girls. She made a king wait and wouldn't let him have her until it was on her terms. Yes, she was eventually beheaded, but she made history.

The most powerful tool with both men and women is the power of no reply. It drives people around the bend. Have you been waiting for a reply to a call, text, or other message for days? You're looking at your phone, at every message, hoping it will be him. An example of this was told to me by my friend who was dating a married guy. He had promised for months that he would leave his wife. He told my friend that he and his wife lived separate lives, that they were only living in the same house for their child and for financial reasons. My friend finally reached her limit. I told her not to reply to any messages; when she was replying, she was sending the message that she was still there waiting in the wings. My friend took my advice. I told her to change her WhatsApp picture of a cartoon character to one of her looking stunning. A mutual friend and I set her up on a blind date, which helped distract her. She didn't reply to him for a week, and on the evening of her blind date, he showed up at her house crying and begging her to give him another chance. Men won't make decisions when they can have their cake and eat it. Until you won't accept anything but being the leading lady, they will treat you like the chorus—part time.

Actions speak louder than words. Don't tell him why you haven't responded. Allow your silence to speak for you. It is a very powerful tool. When you are still in contact, even if it is to say that you are not happy, you are sending the message you are still there. Not replying is a message that translates to "I mean business. I am not just talking the talk—I am showing you that I have reached my limit." I can honestly say that this concept has never failed to work for me or my friends. People have a sixth sense about how far they can push you. Can you remember being a child and knowing when you had pushed a parent too far? Yes, people will push boundaries if you let them. Don't be a supply teacher. If someone has let you down, try silence for a few days; that will have more of an impact than sending reams of text about how hurt you are. When you are ready to talk, I will guarantee you that he will be ready to listen.

"The power of no reply"

LEADING LADY OR CHORUS

Do you want to be the leading lady in your relationship, or do you want to be in the chorus?

I've had an affair, which I regret. There are some situations where people have affairs and then go on to have lifelong relationships. However, men who have long-term affairs seldom leave their wives or partners. If you've been having an affair for longer than six months, it's unlikely that he is going to leave his wife (pied piper concept). Before you know it, a year has passed, and you've invested time and emotions into a relationship that was doomed to fail. Everyone deserves to be the leading lady in her own life. If you're prepared to settle for the chorus, expect him to put someone else first.

I will share a personal experience I had that reinforces this concept. About ten years ago, I met a very handsome, charming guy through work. We immediately clicked. After the first meeting, he gave me his business card. I clasped the card in my hands paired with a wide grin, and I slipped it into my pocket. I left it there for a few days but then texted him. That was the beginning of a few months on the roller coaster. It was amazing, he made me smile and laugh like no one else. He told me he had a grown son. After a while, he told me he was married. I couldn't believe it, but by then I was emotionally attached and involved. The relationship soon ended. I wasn't about to be his fallback girl. Did I read the road signs? When I look back, I know I should have, but he was a professional cheat.

We went out in town where people knew us. I just didn't have any reason to question him.

We stayed in touch over the years with the odd text or fleeting chance meeting at work. While writing this book, we reconnected. I loved his company and didn't see any harm in remaining in touch and having the odd coffee. We had arranged lunch one Friday; I had sent a message saying I had arranged a lift after lunch as I had a family event. The next day he called me and said that he didn't want to meet me if there was a time limit on it—he wanted us to "go with the flow." Now I could see how manipulative he was. He was giving me ultimatums and wanted us to stay out. I said that we were two friends catching up for lunch, and I didn't feel it was necessary to stay out. We left the conversation unresolved. I mulled it over, and the more I thought about it, the more I realised that I had come light years from the person I had been, the person who would get carried away by the pied piper concept. He had wanted me to stay in the hope we would have a few drinks and then one thing would lead to another. This time I read the road signs.

My agenda was lunch with a friend. His agenda was a ride on the roller coaster. I cancelled the meeting. He was the same person I knew ten years ago. He hadn't changed at all. He was still living a double life. He had a family at home and would have affairs if and when there was a willing participant. As charming as he was, I could see the situation for what it was. I told him that friendship was about compromise. I further explained that I had agreed to meet him as a friend because I enjoyed his company and nothing more. It felt amazing to finally be in control and have self-esteem. He was surprised by my response. After a few days, he sent me a message saying that I was right and he was selfish.

This guy was on a teacup ride. He clearly wasn't happy at home. But for his own reasons, be it money or children, he stayed in his situation. Desperate for excitement, he would have short or even long-term flings.

The woman who enters into this type of doomed relationship doesn't realise that her actions keep him in the unhappy marriage. She is also not being fair to the other person in the marriage, who is completely oblivious or who maybe knows but stays for the same reasons. I know this guy is unfulfilled and unhappy, but he is too scared to be with someone who could potentially hurt him, so he stays on his teacup ride. He has a ride on the roller coaster now and then, which makes the teacup ride far easier to be on. But I am now a leading lady, and an affair is never something I will enter into again.

The power comes with recognising the situation, just as I did. My concepts are codes for people to understand psychological behaviours—titles to recognise when you are going down a certain path.

I experienced another situation that I am not proud of. I met a guy through work who was engaged to be married. We had become close over the time that we had worked together. When we were suddenly separated, I mistook the separation for something else, and I thought I was in love. The guy got married. We tried to stay away from each other, but eventually something happened between us. I was clear with him from the start that I wasn't going to have an affair, and, after only six weeks of marriage, he left his wife to enter into a relationship with me. We were together for about eighteen months. In the beginning it was fantastic, but as the reality and guilt set in, the relationship became toxic.

I won't and don't do affairs, however, in the eyes of society I was the bad guy. Let's remember, I was single. I didn't have a child and I hadn't married anyone, but men don't get the bad press, women do. I didn't know his wife. She wasn't my friend, and therefore I had no loyalty to her. Why would I? If there was one thing I could change in my life, it would be that one thing. I am not proud of getting involved with someone who was married, but I wouldn't have engaged in that relationship had he not left. I wouldn't see him unless he was single, so he left. That one bad decision follows me around like a shadow. It was a work relationship, and it changed people's opinion of me. People couldn't understand or grasp the fact that he had left.

The facts are that my concepts work. I am a leading lady, and I won't be the chorus—that's where most women fall down. Making it clear that I wouldn't have an affair forced made him make decisions.

The guilt got to be too much. I wanted to end the relationship sooner, but I felt obligated to stay with him as he had given up everything to explore a relationship with me. What did I do wrong? It's girl code—I shouldn't have gotten involved. However, you have to ask how right the relationship was before I came on the scene; happily married people don't leave their home for no reason.

I ended the relationship, changed my mobile number, and didn't look back. He went back to his wife, and they now have another child. I feel some sort of peace knowing that they worked through things. What amazes me is that I am the bad guy, the vixen, the bad person. He is forgiven and welcomed back to the fold. Is that fair? Hell no, it's not fair. He gets a pat on the back from the guys, and I get scowls from the girls and bad press from the guys. This needs to change. The only person who had any obligation to his wife was him. I admit it was incredibly bad timing, and I accept that I should have stayed away, however, I am human, and we all make mistakes. Feelings can be powerful and can cloud our judgment. If someone you felt strongly about had left his situation to be with you and was honest about it, would you turn him away for another woman (his wife) who you didn't know? Who he maintained he didn't want to be with? Be honest and think about that. The problem is that in situations like this, women are always the enemy.

Our attitudes need to change. If that same situation was to happen to me, I would ask questions like, "Why has this happened? Where did things go wrong?" I would hold my partner responsible, not the other woman, as he has the relationship with me not her. It's the same with women who sleep with lots of men; they are branded whores, but a guy is just a player and gets admiration from his peers.

We talk about equality, but seldom do we support the women who are getting called out for doing what men do. Seldom do we criticise the man who has cheated on his wife—straight away it's that the woman is a home wrecker. A relationship that can be destroyed by another woman is not the kind of relationship I would want to be in. It's always easier to blame a third party than it is to look at yourself and ask difficult questions.

Affairs happen every day. The aim of this book is to ensure you are in the minority—that you are not in the majority of women who settle for the wrong man for the wrong reason. I have shared my own personal story because it was one of the most difficult times of my life. If I could go back I would change it, I would not follow the same path again. I hurt a lot of people and it's something I deserve to be criticised for. I am owning it and taking responsibility for my actions. We can't change the past but we can change the future and learn from our mistakes.

"Be the leading lady not the chorus"

THINK LIKE A TEN

No matter what shape or size you are, think like a ten. Make yourself think you are a ten, and you will be. When you go to work and you're given a job, think like a ten: you've got this. When you step out to go on that date, think like a ten. You are a ten out of ten, and you can do anything. When you're walking down the street, think like a ten, and act like a ten, and you will be a ten. The key to confidence starts with how you think. It's your choice: you can walk down the street with your head down, or you can walk with confidence and purpose. I have heard so many men talk about women, saying it's how they carry themselves or that they just have something about them. That's called thinking like a ten. I have to add that the men who have gotten my attention weren't always the best-looking guys, but they thought they were a ten, and so I believed they were a ten! Being a ten is choice; it's a state of mind. If I ever had to do presentations at work, I would think of someone I thought was amazing at it, and I would think like they would: I was a ten. They say the antidote to fear is confidence. Make confidence your state of mind in everything you do. If you're not happy with how someone has treated you, ask yourself if a ten would be happy with the situation. Would a ten put up with it? So why should you put up with it? Let that be your benchmark.

Most people who are public speakers admit to being nervous before they go out on stage. The great thing about this is that you would never know it. It's the same with comedians. What makes them funny is their confidence and delivery.

There was a famous man in America who committed fraud. He convinced airline pilots that he was an airline pilot; he went on to convince doctors—professional, educated people—that he was a doctor when he had absolutely no medical background. My point is that you can be whatever you want to be—it's a state of mind. If you think and act with confidence, it will translate. You don't need to study for years; you don't need money, and you can't buy it. You don't need to be a certain shape or size. You just need to change how you think. You decide. It's your choice. No excuses. No "I don't have enough money" or "I am not clever enough." That does not matter. It's about reprogramming your belief system and making the conscious decision to believe in yourself.

The next time you feel bad about something or think to yourself that you need to lose weight or that you can't do something, think of the things you do like about yourself and focus on them. Change gears. You are in control. Every time you start to feel negative about something, be aware of it, and use this concept. The only barrier is you.

Have you seen an experiment where people are asked to taste wine, for example, but the labels are covered so that the person doesn't know what they are drinking? There is usually a cheap brand and an expensive brand. They ask ten people which one they prefer, and then they show them what they are drinking. Often, the majority are surprised to discover that what they preferred was the cheaper brand. When the experiment is conducted with a new group of people with the brand revealed, the results are different—the name brand comes out on top. It is all about perception. If you were a brand, what brand would you be? You can project whatever brand you want. If you engage with confidence, people will perceive you as confident.

EMPTY RESTAURANT CONCEPT

Play hard to get. It's an old cliché, but it works—ask any man; ask any woman—if you have to work for it, you must want it. It's human nature and universal. No one can escape it.

A friend of mine was dating a wealthy, successful man who was used to women throwing themselves at his feet. They were yes girls. I told her to be the opposite of what he was used to. Some might say that that's not being yourself, however, sometimes it's necessary. She would never have gotten his attention had she not used a few tactics. I told her to think, dress and act like a ten. I have dated airline captains, dentists and doctors, and I found that the more professional they are, the more they are used to having women being readily available to them and not being a challenge because they are seduced by their occupation and status. Think about it, these men are ambitious—or they wouldn't have got to where they are in life. Do you think that needy women who are all over them will turn them on? If you do, wake up and smell the coffee. Think outside the box. The nice girl never wins the race. It's hard to hear but true. I am not saying spend your whole life playing games, but sometimes you may need a tool bag of skills to get that guy to notice you.

Centuries ago, men hunted for food. It is in their blood to hunt and chase. In the world of dating, there are tools you can use to get the attention of that man you so desire. My advice is this: be a challenge. Don't reply the second after he texts you. Don't say, "I'm free every night this week," say, "I have one night available," and if he can't make it, let him wait longer. He will soon make himself available. It works. My friend is now married to that guy and they have an amazing life together. She did what every woman had failed to do before her. She did everything they didn't. She made him work for it. She wasn't available at the drop of a hat. He knew if he wanted to see her he had to give her notice or she would just have something else on her schedule. But, more importantly, she acted like his equal. She wasn't fazed by his high-powered job or wealth, and she focused on the things that make us all equal: personality, charm, intelligence, and humour.

If you act like a ten, he will believe you are. If you act like a five, he will see you as just that.

Have you ever tried booking a table at an exclusive restaurant? You were unable to because it's already booked up? You are left feeling disappointed. The next time you want to book there you make sure you book in advance. It's the same with people, don't be available all of the time. Don't be that empty restaurant, be the one people are booking in advance to visit. I have a friend who runs her own business, when clients contact her for an appointment she will always make them wait even if she has availability. It sends the message 'this person is busy and booked up so they must be good,' further it makes the person want the appointment more. When something is sold out or not in stock, most of us will go out of our way to find it. Apply this tactic to your dating life.

"Don't be the empty restaurant"

MONEY DOESN'T MAKE YOU BETTER

One of my friends avoids successful and wealthy men; she says she feels intimidated by them. Try to put such things aside and see others as just people not as their job or status. Most people are different people in their home life than they are in their work life. Everyone, regardless of his or her status, is looking for love. If you put wealth aside and concentrate on the person, there will always be a level playing field. Remember, wealthy people often have a different problem—wondering if someone is with them for who they are or for the lifestyle they can offer. In love we are all equal; so forget what he has and look at him as a person. A big bank balance doesn't make him good in bed or funny, and a high-powered job doesn't mean he's a better person. It's important to remind yourself of this in the world of dating and relationships.

Don't be fazed by wealth and power because they aren't the things that the soul is made up of. Cars and fancy jewellery won't keep you warm at night. Remember, he may have all that, but what he is looking for is someone to share it with. Money is nothing without love. So remember, when you feel you might not be good enough for him because you're not loaded, you are more than good enough. Wealth doesn't make your heart swell, and that feeling is something that money can't buy. He might be able to fly to Niagara Falls, but what does that mean without that special person to be there with him and share the moment?

Keep these things in mind if you ever feel like my friend does when around very successful men. Don't rule anyone out for reasons such as this. Behind the fancy cars and clothes is a person just like you and me.

DON'T SHOW THE WHOLE FILM, ONLY THE TRAILER

When getting to know a guy, don't tell him everything about you on the first few dates. Don't tell him about your failed relationships, and don't tell him you've been counting down the days until you next see him. Don't tell him you've googled your star-sign compatibility. Why watch the film if someone has told you the whole plot? Be mysterious. Keep him guessing a little. Show him a preview so that he will want to watch the whole movie.

A friend of mine is into unconventional things like mediums and alternative healing. Not everyone will get things like that, especially on a first date. Of course, it's about being yourself, but most men are going to find it a little odd if you're going on about ethereal spirits on the first date instead of alcohol spirits! Choose your audience. You can talk to your friends about that sort of thing and eventually include him if things progress.

My friend would wonder why there wasn't a second date. The topic was important to her but not to the guy she had just met! My friend is amazing, but potential suitors were scared off by something they simply didn't understand. It may sound harsh, but it's the truth. Even though most people are open-minded, save those conversations for later down the line.

This also applies in the physical element of the relationship. As I mentioned in guideline number 6, do not show the whole movie on the first night!

"Don't show the whole film, only the trailer"

TENNIS GAME

This is the sister concept to 'Don't Show the Whole Film, Only the Trailer'. Another friend I have can't help it: she has to tell her dates her life story. That is a big no-no. Have you ever been on a date or met someone new and had to sit there, pretending you were interested in his or her life story? A date needs to be an exchange—like tennis. If one person has the ball for too long, the other person gets bored or loses interest. It needs to be a two-way conversation, where both share information. Have some questions ready to ask just in case you feel nervous or feel that you are doing all the talking. Keep it like a game of tennis, back and forth, with both people having to think and, more importantly, to communicate. Don't concentrate on it too much—a date should be fun and natural. Just be self-aware; you'll be surprised how effective it can be. Don't hold the ball too long before you give it back!

I have been on dates where men have talked about their exes, which is a big red flag. Talking about your ex on a first date signals "I am not over my ex. He [or she] still affects me so much that I've brought him [or her] to the date!" That's a big turn off. If you find yourself doing that, I would say that you aren't ready to date. Of course, over time you will discuss your past, but no man or woman wants to hear about your ex on the first date. Common sense, you may think. However, you would be amazed how this topic trickles into the conversation. Give him a taste of your humour, a taste of your sexiness; keep the conversation lighthearted and not too heavy.

No one wants to hear your life story on the first date—or the second or the third for that matter! Unfold like a book with chapters. Can you imagine reading a book that has the whole plot in the first chapter? Why read on? It's the same with people. Dating should be fun while you slowly get to know each other.

NEVER SHOW YOUR HAND

I know people may disagree with this, but it's one of the concepts I am most passionate about. Who wants to play a game of cards with someone if you know their hand? People will say, "I'm not into playing games." Whatever. Let me tell you, life is one big game. We play games every day. We are playing games when we go to work and put on a brave face when our personal life is falling apart. We are playing games when someone asks, "How are you?" and you reply, "Great," knowing that it's a lie. Never show all your cards—keep a few close to your chest. It keeps a relationship exciting and keeps men on their toes. Men like a challenge. They are competitive. Keep them guessing a little. It will drive them crazy.

A friend of mine was dating a new guy. In the beginning, he did all the chasing. He'd take her out for champagne lunches. However, the dynamic quickly changed. My friend had showed all her cards. She had laid her soul bare, and it killed the spark, the challenge, and the fun! She became needy and would tell him how she felt if he didn't call. Dating suicide. He stopped replying and completely withdrew, which made her lose her balance and behave in ways all women (and men) dread. My friend did the drive-by! Cut off with no real explanation, she went on a quest for answers. My friend was caught by one of his neighbours when driving past his house. Although we had hours of laughter over the incident, it made her look completely irrational, which she isn't. How could the dynamics have changed from champagne lunches to no reply?

They changed because she had laid all her cards on the table in a very short period of time. In the beginning, she was fun and a challenge, but she very quickly changed. Men want a challenge; men like you to keep them guessing. There is a right time to show your cards and a right person to show them to—but not straight away.

THE BALLERINA CONCEPT

Even if you enjoy being kept on your toes, no one wants to be a ballerina.

It's good and healthy to be kept on your toes in a relationship. It keeps it exciting. That said avoid the relationships where you are constantly on your toes—the result will be bleeding feet. You'll spend more time tending to your wounds than enjoying the relationship. The ballerina concept is when you constantly worry about what he is doing or who he is texting. He's putting you down, making you feel insecure, and it's a long way back to rebuild your confidence. Be a friend to yourself.

A friend of mine started dating a guy who, in the beginning, seemed fantastic. However, as time progressed, we all noticed a huge change in her. My friend became obsessed with her weight and appearance. It transpired that the reason for her dramatic weight loss was because her partner was going on about his ex-girlfriend all the time—how great and slim she was. This had a negative effect on my friend. She would barely eat when we were out. Her clothes were hanging off her. Although she seemed delighted with her weight loss, this was an unhealthy relationship. My friend was constantly on her toes, worrying about her appearance and feeling insecure about his ex-girlfriend. It was a classic ballerina concept: my friend spent most of her days worrying and comparing herself to his ex-girlfriend. A partner should bring out the best in you, not actively try to make you feel insecure. Look out for the ballerinas, always on their toes.

"We all like to be kept on our toes, but you should never become a ballerina"

NEVER GIVE UP YOUR
LIFE FOR A MAN

So many women make the mistake of giving up their interests and friends for a man. This never works. Doing everything to please your partner has the opposite effect. Men like independent women with their own interests.

A guy I worked with was very attractive and incredibly popular with the women. He could snap his fingers and get a date with most girls. One girl turned down a date with him; she was in a running club and wouldn't miss it. He couldn't believe it! He wasn't used to a woman putting her own life before his. That girl got his attention more than any girl I had seen before. Why? Because she had her own life. She wasn't about to put her life on hold for a date with a guy. What message did that send to him? "Wow, I'm going to have to up my game with this girl." The attractive women he had dated only kept his interest for so long. She wasn't like every other girl he had dated. It is hard to say no when you meet someone and love spending time with him, but never miss a date with your friends or a date with your interests for a guy.

MONKEY SEE, MONKEY DO

Men don't listen to women nagging—they just hear noise. My friend's husband was very controlling. He did what he liked and when he liked. On one occasion, he tested her to the limit. He went out and got so drunk that he passed out at his brother's house and didn't come home. If she had done that to him he would have been furious! I told her not to nag and to just say she was disappointed. I suggested that she wait a few weeks and then do it back. My friend agreed. The result was seventeen missed calls and a doting husband. Oh yes, it worked all right. Trust me—it works with every man. Remember the supply-teacher concept? If you're going to be the supply teacher, expect him to push your boundaries. If it happens to you, try monkey see, monkey do. If it's good for the goose, it's good for the gander.

Another friend was reluctant to come away on a girls' weekend. I encouraged her to come, and it worked wonders. Upon her return from the trip, she called me to say that her boyfriend had done all the annoying jobs around the house that she had been badgering him about, and he had booked them a surprise week away for the following month! Men need to be reminded every now and again of what they have, and a weekend away is the perfect way of doing just that.

FLIP THE COIN

It seems to be a tale as old as time, women worrying about other women. Women worrying about how they will look in their bikini. How many times has a guy made you feel insecure about your body or sat there with his friends going on about women's breasts or making other personal comments? It's time to flip the coin and do it back. I don't mean in a malicious way. For example, I posted a picture of David Gandy on Instagram. None of my married friends liked the picture. I'm assuming it was because they didn't want to hurt their partner's feelings. I think it's time that women kept men on their toes, let them worry about how they look on the beach for a change. There is nothing wrong with healthy competition ladies, but there is something wrong if you can't say a guy is hot.

What's good for the goose is good for the gander. Flip the coin, ladies. It doesn't always have to be one-sided. Don't compromise yourself—compromise with others. It's all about balance. A little spice added to a meal once in a while definitely heats things up! A weekend away with the girls works wonders. Don't stop seeing your friends when you're in a relationship. Trust me. You need your friends if and when things go wrong.

You never hear a guy referring to Mary Poppins as the woman of his dreams. Be the bad girl once in a while. Men love a little bit of a bad girl, just as we like a little bit of a bad boy. Keep them on their toes—don't let yourself get too comfortable.

The wife of a friend of mine at work was going away on a girls' weekend. As a couple, their relationship was losing its spark. Between the kids and work, things had gotten very mundane. He had started texting other women. I remember him saying to me that his wife was going away; it had definitely gotten him thinking. I was secretly thinking that it would do him good.

At a conversation over lunch, he told me that his wife had said that she didn't feel right about leaving him and the kids all weekend, and she was thinking of cancelling. My friend said to me, "I wish she would go! Maybe the space would do us good."

This was coming from a guy. There it was, right in front of me: the flickering flame that was struggling to stay lit had just had water thrown on it!

The worst thing his wife could have done was to appear needy and put her own life on hold. His wife had become boring and predictable. Just because you're married or have children doesn't mean you can't have fun and a life too. I have seen relationships take a three hundred and sixty-degree turn when the woman's starts going out and having new interests. When all your life consists of is your children and husband, you become needy and dependent. Is that the person you were when he married you? You're not just a mother and wife; you are your own person too.

How many times have you seen a woman go through a breakup, and, all of a sudden, she's at the gym, she's buying new clothes, and she's going out. And then—bingo!—the ex-boyfriend is interested again and asking her back. We do the same with men. How many times have you looked at an ex and thought, "Why didn't he do that when he was with me?"

Why wait for things to go wrong to do this?

BEAUTY IS IN THE EYE
OF THE BEHOLDER

Attraction is very complex. You don't have to be size zero to be attractive. In every magazine we look at, there is almost always an article on how to lose weight—or pictures of celebrities being criticised for their weight gain. I have a friend who is a size eighteen, and she is the life and soul of every party. She is amazing company, and men fall at her feet. The attraction with her is the way she carries herself. Confidence is the key to most things. When the world sees these things as attractive, more so than the physical makeup we are born with, we will have more confident women. There are many desirable women with gifts beyond a physical appearance: successful women, funny women, kind women, strong women, and intelligent women. These are the qualities that get women dates and, more importantly—the missing piece of their jigsaw—a marriage proposal to the man of their dreams. So don't think that just because you don't look like a supermodel you won't meet Mr. Right.

I have to share a story with you that really reinforces this idea. I have a male friend who I talk to about very personal things. He told me this story. When he was in his teen years, he met a girl called Jane. They dated for a while but lost touch when they left school. He went on to meet Sarah, who he married. While married to Sarah, he bumped into Jane again, and their connection was undeniable. They embarked on an affair. Something happened that he wasn't expecting: both women became pregnant at the same time. He had to tell his wife about Jane and the affair. From that day forward, his relationship with his wife broke down, as you can well imagine. He eventually left and started a new life with Jane. They married and were happy for many years. But their relationship broke down after fifteen years, and he met Angela, who he is currently with and has been with for the past fourteen years.

I asked him which woman was the love of his life. Even though he is currently happy with Angela, he said Jane. He said that one of his friends had asked him, "If Angela and Jane were hanging off a cliff, which one would you save?" He had said it would have to be Jane. I asked to see a picture of them both. Angela was slim, attractive, and well-dressed. Jane was a larger lady and, in the eyes of society, not as physically attractive as Angela. The moral of the story is that love and attraction are about a deeper connection. He loved Jane, and even after ten years with Angela, Jane had his heart. Never underestimate how powerful a connection can be. I asked him why he felt that way, and he said there was a spark between them that could never die. The physical side of their relationship had been amazing. The spark and connection didn't have a price. So for the women who don't feel they will meet their dream man because they aren't what society deems as perfect, remember this story and have faith in that connection, a soul connection.

FALLBACK GIRL

The fallback girl is the girl who has affairs, the girl who will be the booty call, the girl who men will call so that they can have their cake and eat it too. An example of the fallback girl is a friend of mine who was having an affair with a married man. He would come to her house, and they would drink wine and have great sex, but then he would go back to his wife and wake up with his wife in the morning. He would spend quality time with his wife, be there to carry her shopping bags, rub her feet after a hard day, and financially support her. Why would you be happy to be the part-time lover? Why would you sell yourself short? The fallback girl keeps the guy's marriage alive. He won't make any decisions while he is having his cake and eating it too.

Another example of the fallback girl is the girl who will be the booty call, who will allow herself to be used. When the guy has nothing better going on, she will get the call. The fallback girls strokes the guy's ego, and he uses her when he wants sex or when he is bored. The fallback girl doesn't meet his parents or anyone important. The fallback girl doesn't get breakfast in bed. She is the woman he leans on and falls back on when there is nothing else available. Are you a fallback girl? Remember the earlier concept, leading lady or chorus? You deserve nothing less than being the leading lady in your life.

LIMBO LAND

Limbo land is that place where you are stuck when you haven't made a decision on what to do or where you are going. It's the worst place to be.

A male friend of mine had been married over twenty years, and the relationship had become like that of a brother and sister. He met someone else, and this girl was a lot younger. He was in torment about his decision. I told him that his torment would end once he made a decision.

When we are spending lots of time mulling over a decision, we are in limbo land.

Limbo land is a place where we are stagnant, not moving forward, not going anywhere. Rest assured, whatever the choices or decisions are that you are mulling over, once you have made the decision you will feel 100 percent better. Take control. Don't wait around for choices to be made for you.

Another friend of mine met a guy who lived overseas. He often travelled with his work to the United Kingdom, so there was a realistic chance of a relationship. The guy was very attentive, showering her with attention, but then, suddenly, he cut her off. We thought that something had happened to him as he just didn't respond to calls and texts. She eventually called him from a withheld number to see if he was alive. He most certainly was. She simply hung up. My friend had just wanted closure, and she now knew he was choosing to ignore her.

We spent weeks coming up with ideas as to why he had suddenly had a change of heart; eventually my friend put it to bed. A year later she received a text from him. He asked how she was, saying how sorry he was for how he'd left things. He said that he was in a bad place and had been thinking about her and would like to meet up. After an hour-long conversation with us girls, she decided to give him another chance. He began texting regularly, asking her which restaurant to book and sending her videos of him and his friends at a party. And then—boom!—no contact for days. Where was my friend now? She was in limbo land, that horrible place where you don't know where you are with someone. You wonder what's happening between you. Are you meeting up again? It's horrible. My friend had gone from being all excited about the prospect of dating again to limbo land—it was the same cycle, the same behaviour. I told her to make a decision and cut him off.

This time she did. He had had her down as the supply teacher, and, from his behaviour, I'm guessing that he had someone else in the background. He used my friend and the female attention as a distraction and to boost his self-esteem.

Limbo land is a place where you're being messed around. You're in limbo. Your life is suspended; you feel bad; and you don't know where you stand. Take control and get a ticket out of there. It's your choice. Make a decision or wait around for weeks until someone makes it for you.

INDICATE, MIRROR, SIGNAL, MANOEUVRE

You wouldn't pull out of an intersection without letting someone know where you are going. You indicate your intention and then pull out when it's safe to do so. It's the same with people and life. Don't expect people to be able to read your mind. Put yourself out there, and give off the right signals, because we all know, when you think someone is turning left and you pull out, accidents happen.

Body language forms a huge percentage of non-verbal communication (NVC) and is so important. Sometimes men need a signal. Don't be afraid to put yourself out there. Many women fear rejection. However, there are ways of sending the right signals to get what you want, be it rejection or an invitation.

Many of us judge others without looking at our own behaviour. You may go home after a night out and wonder why your friend got approached by lots of men and you didn't. Are you approachable? What signals are you giving off? Is it "Don't come near me!"? Think about how you come across. Next time you're in a bar, people watch. Observe who you think is approachable and why. Remember, when you're in a bar on a night out, a guy isn't going to approach you if you don't indicate, just as anyone wouldn't pull out of an intersection. Smile. Give eye contact. Be approachable. Send the right signals.

A very attractive friend of mine would moan about never being approached by men. I asked her if she would approach a male version of her. She laughed and said that she had never thought of it that way. Think of it, ladies, because it can be the difference between your dream guy approaching you or him leaving without getting a chance to meet you.

UNPLUG THE SOURCE

You're crying over your ex-boyfriend. You're engaging in constant texts, getting drawn into arguments. Before you know it, you're meeting up with him, and the same cycle starts all over again. If we want the lights off, we turn a switch. I know emotions are not quite that simple, but you have the power to unplug the electricity supply; you have the power to turn off the light. If someone is causing you pain, you have the power to stop further pain by removing yourself from the source. Unplug them. Remember, you have the power to do that. When we are living in the past, we can never live in the here and now.

For example, if you got badly sunburned, would you go back out in the sun the next day? You would stay away from the sun and protect yourself. It's no different with emotional pain. Think about the damage you are doing to your emotional well-being. Why would you go back to a situation that hurt you? Did it not hurt you enough? It's something to think about.

When you remove yourself from a bad situation, you are getting a piece of yourself back with every hour that passes. It's like plugging your charger back into yourself. Taking the lead out that is draining your battery. Be aware of the energy source that you are plugged into. Surround yourself with a positive energy source.

A GOOD GAMBLER KNOWS WHEN TO QUIT

Have you ever gambled? Most of the time the rush of winning encourages people to gamble the money they've won. If we continue rolling the dice, we can end up losing everything.

I equate this to power within relationships. I will share an example of this concept from a male perspective. A male friend of mine had been dating a girl for about five months, I had never seen him so smitten with anyone the way he was with this woman. He announced he was taking her to Spain to meet his father, I knew this was a huge deal for him. I waited in anticipation to hear all about the weekend.

As we sat down to catch up, I could see he wasn't himself and asked how the weekend had gone. He explained that on the first night they had a huge row. That evening they were due to attend a family gathering. They never got to the party together. During the argument she left the bar where they were having pre party drinks and told him to attend the function alone. She returned to the hotel room and refused to go. He described how he was so annoyed that he had taken her all that way to meet his family that he didn't go after her, and left her in the hotel room all night alone! I broke into a nervous laugh, because I knew that most probably didn't go down very well.

He explained the following day she had ended the relationship and he was dumb founded by her response. I told him I wouldn't have been happy being left alone in a hotel room for the night! He said he couldn't run after her as with most arguments he felt he was in the right. He was also very stubborn. A few days went by and he made contact with her with a view to resolving the matter. However, she was still very distant and seemed certain about her decision. He was in turmoil, he wasn't used a woman standing up to him and being so strong. He left it a week or so and tried again to reach out to her and try and resolve the matter, she still wouldn't engage with him.

After about a month his attitude changed he told me he wouldn't contact her again. After about five weeks she made contact with him in an attempt to rekindle the relationship. Unfortunately by this time he felt she had taken things too far. She had gambled and lost.

My friend needed a woman who would stand up to him otherwise the relationship wouldn't have worked. That had been the very reason he had liked her so much. When she stood her ground the next day she did just that. Initially he was annoyed however by standing her ground they established boundaries. He knew how far he could push her and vise-versa. If she had of withdrawn for a few days or even a week she would have had him in the palm of her hand, but she carried the argument on which resulted in him losing interest and moving on.

The message is, know when to cash in your chips, know when it's time to stop rolling the dice. It's important to stand your ground in relationships but it's equally important to know when to let something go or call a truce. There was a power struggle within this relationship, which resulted in both losing. Holding onto bad feeling and bring up past issues is unhealthy, learn to let the small things go.

REASON, SEASON, OR LIFETIME?

An old lady I knew once said this, and it stuck with me: some people are in your life for a reason, some for only a season, and some will be there for a lifetime. I can really relate to this. Just because you had a relationship and it didn't last doesn't mean it was any less special than the ones you have had that will last a lifetime. Some relationships we have are there just for us to learn from the experience—and some provide more learning than others. Some relationships are like shooting stars, beautiful but short-lived. People will come and go from your life, but I believe there is a reason for all relationships. The bad ones are often a mirror, showing us our own reflection. We sometimes see things about ourselves that we don't like. The key is to accept that relationships come and go, and sometimes they are not meant to last a lifetime. If you were to get a pen and paper and write down all your relationships, I can guarantee they will all have one thing in common: one of you will have learned something. The message is to value them all, because they all have something to offer you. You just might not know it yet.

RED WOLF

There are many different colours of wolves—brown, black, white, and those that seem a mixture of all of those shades. There are also red wolves, which are less common and seldom seen but you can discover if you travel places to find them.

I have always felt like the red wolf, I was always different. I have often felt that I didn't fit in, even as far back as primary school. My mum was German, and I had a different name. Being so different was hard as a child. And although those are differences that I now love, it wasn't easy growing up.

If you are reading this book and wondering if you will ever meet anyone you really like again, let me let you in on a secret: patience is the key. You are unique. For me, finding my soul mate is like finding another red wolf.

It's the same with friends. I didn't fit in with the usual crowds. I didn't have a huge circle of friends, but when I did meet another like-minded person, it was a very special experience. I am different, so not everyone will get me. You may go on ten dates and not feel a connection with any of them. It doesn't mean there is anything wrong with you; it just means you haven't met the right guy yet. I have listened to so many women who are feeling pressure because they are dating and haven't met anyone they have liked or who has liked them.

It will take longer for some to find their soul mate. We are all unique. Some they are happy to settle with just someone and go with the flow.

Never be disheartened. It may take you a long time to find your soul mate because not everyone might get you—and vice-versa. Don't think there is something wrong with you because you have been single awhile and a friend has met someone straight away. It's not a reflection on you. Just be patient. When you do meet your red wolf—that like-minded person—it will be worth the wait.

LIVING IN THE MOMENT

It is very cliché, I know, but I have spent endless hours listening to both men and women not making the choices they really want to make for fear of being hurt. The fear of something happening is far worse than the reality. Fear makes you a prisoner in your own life. They say the antidote to fear is confidence. Have you ever been in a relationship where you were insecure and spent most of your time worrying about the worst thing happening—about someone prettier coming along or about it not working out because he is too young or too old? It's wasted energy and stops us from enjoying the present. All we have is now, this moment. So live in the moment. Be present in the moment because the future isn't here yet. What we most fear doesn't destroy us; it's the thought of what could go wrong that does. Let go, and enjoy this moment. Time waits for no one. The here and now are all we can be sure of.

If you want to meet your dream guy, take action. Do something about it. Push yourself, and step out of your comfort zone. Going on dates builds up your confidence. It's not the easiest thing to do. It can be scary, but it's all learning and experience. I spoke with a male friend at work who had been single for six years. I asked him why he didn't join a dating site. He told me that one of the main things that put him off was the stigma attached to it and that people at work would know he was on a dating site. Other people and what they might think had held him back from doing something he wanted to do. Have conviction in what you do. Everyone is single at one time in his or her life. Don't let other people's opinions matter more than your own. What's the worst that could happen? A few people might be making comments. Does it really matter what they think? Are they that important? And are they more important than your happiness?

THE EMPEROR'S NEW CLOTHES

The Emperor's New Clothes is my all-time favorite children's book. For those who don't know the story, I will enlighten you. The emperor wanted some new clothes made for a parade. He was approached by two fraudsters who agreed to make him clothes out of invisible thread. They held up their hands in the air, holding nothing, and asked the emperor to try on the clothes. The tailors tell the emperor that those who are stupid or not worthy of their positions will not be able to see the clothes. The emperor pretends that he can see these imaginary clothes as he doesn't want to look stupid. In the end, he walks in his parade naked. It is obvious to everyone that he is naked, yet no one person will admit to it for fear of seeming stupid or unworthy.

I equate this story to women who go along with the most ridiculous situations and believe the most silly excuses and stories. Have you ever been listening to a girlfriend talk about her relationship and wonder how can she believe what she is saying? How can she not see what's right in front of her?! Of course you have. But you don't want to be the one who points out the obvious. I call this the emperor's new clothes.

A friend of mine, by her own admission, is in the wrong relationship. We learned her partner had been seeing other women. Even with the knowledge of this and his poor behaviour, she would get back with him. Eventually she would convince herself it was nothing, only harmless banter, and almost justify his behaviour. I would listen and think she was wearing the emperor's new clothes. She, just like the emperor, was being conned and made a fool of. Look out for this concept, don't be afraid to challenge something when you know it's not right. Don't conform out of fear of being rejected, if something sounds too good to be true or seems hard to believe it most probably is. Be honest and true to yourself.

DO WE EVER REALLY KNOW SOMEONE?

I will share a story with you that really pulled on my heartstrings. A woman, who I will refer to as Mandy, met her husband Paul when they were very young. They became childhood sweethearts, were married, bought their home for peanuts and went on to have four children.

One morning she awoke to a knock on the door. It was a man who claimed he had been in a relationship with her husband many years.

Devastated, and in complete shock her world would never be the same again. The marriage broke down and her family torn apart. The house she had bought thirty years ago, which she thought she'd see her last days in, was now up for sale. How could this have happened?

It turned out her husband had been leading a double life for many years. He struggled with his sexuality and tried to conform by leading the conventional married life. She was unaware of the situation, and, as a result, she had lost her home and felt her whole life had been a lie. That is an extreme example, but I believe life offers road signs to let us know where we are going. If she was to be honest, had she read the road signs?

A recent documentary portrayed a very famous person, now in his sixties, who now wants to change his sex to be a woman. I think it's amazing. He decided to be true to himself. My point is, looking back now, were there road signs? Of course there were, but we make a choice to read those signs or to drive by and ignore them.

That little voice that speaks to you when you turn the lights out is the truest friend you have—it's called instinct. If you have a feeling something just isn't right, trust it. If you know the relationship is no longer right for you, when your head hits the pillow, you will know. We all have the answers to our own questions; we just have to ask ourselves the questions instead of asking others.

It also highlights how important it is to not conform and be true to yourself. People's lives can be devastated by our choice to try and fit in. No one can criticise a person for being who they are. However, as we have seen from the above scenario, lives can be torn apart, when you try and fit in to the box society has made for us.

LIFE IS SHORT

Somebody somewhere is making a coffin and preparing a speech about someone's life. One day, someone will be preparing a speech about your life. This is fact. So live life for you. Don't be treated in any other way than how you should be treated. Aim for the stars. Make a bucket list. As I've said before, time waits for no one. This is not a rehearsal; this is the real thing. Life is certainly too short to settle for second best. The months and years fly by, and when I am on my deathbed, I want to be able to say I lived and reached my fullest potential.

Don't waste a minute of your life, because, one day, minutes are all you will have left. Make that bucket list today. Never settle for that guy because he is safe, settle for the guy who treats you like a princess. Even if it takes years to meet the right person, a few amazing years with the right man are better than years with the wrong man. Make being single an adventure, think of the amazing people you could meet.

FIND THE RIGHT RECEPTOR

The right person is the missing piece to your jigsaw, the plug that fits the socket and supplies you with energy. Not everyone will get you, and not everyone will have your sense of humour, but if you follow your interests, they will more than likely lead you to the right receptor—the person who is right for you, who gets you, and who sees you.

How annoying is a light that flickers when the bulb isn't quite in its socket? People are like that; when you find your right receptor, there will be no flickers—it will just work. I can relate to this concept, I spent many years with a lovely guy, however there was something missing. I couldn't tell you what it was, there was just something that didn't fit right. Don't compromise because eventually that flickering light is something you might, just learn to live with.

DOES HE HAVE YOUR MANUAL?

Finding a soul mate is like finding someone who has your instruction manual. He knows exactly how to communicate with you. He doesn't need parenting or for you to tell him how you expect to be treated. He knows exactly what to do and what to say. It just works.

Your soul mate will know how to put you in your place in such a way that it will keep you in check. It's as if he has read a manual on you! Everything, from furniture to electronical devices, seems to come with a manual. People are complex, and when your soul mate comes along and understands how you work, the relationship will work.

Your soul mate will bring out the best in you. If you need batteries, he will know; if you need a polish, he will know. Your soul mate will laugh when you laugh, cry when you cry. A soul mate has your guidebook, your instructions, and although amazing, it can also be very scary.

With a soul mate, you will feel vulnerable, as it works both ways. They have the power to make you feel fantastic, but they also know all your weaknesses. You have to let go and enjoy both the good and the bad. Your manual contains your deepest fears, your darkest secrets, your insecurities, and your childhood—your core. It's a scary thought to know that someone has all that information about you and knows how you tick.

A soul mate comes with a price, but it is one that most of us are willing to pay. What is the alternative? The teacup ride—a life of safety, of not being hurt. That's not living at all. Be prepared for both sides of meeting the person who has your instruction manual.

IF YOU LOOK TOO HARD, YOU DON'T FIND IT

How annoying is this? But I believe it is true. Life is all about timing, and we all get our moment. But if you look too hard for something, there is no balance. Of course, you have to put yourself out there, but find a balance. It's like trying to grow something under artificial light—forced and not natural. Things should be organic. Patience is the key, and waiting for your right time and your right moment is what makes it all worthwhile. Have fun with life and dating. Don't think the first guy you go on a date with will be Mr. Right. You will know.

It's just like when you try on a dress and know you're buying it, or when you hear a song, love it, and know you will play it over and over. You just know when it's right. You also know when it's not right, so don't force it. Let your relationships be organic, not artificial. The key is not to focus on it too much. It's about getting a life, not just getting a man.

WHAT BOOK ARE YOU?

When you look at your own life and then you look at the lives your friends who are married, do you ever think, "Why couldn't I have met my dream man at twenty-one and lived happily ever after?"

That's all great, but if lives were books, mine would be an interesting read. True, I didn't meet the man of my dreams at twenty-one, but I have had a hell of a ride on the roller coaster—I never was one for the teacup ride. What book are you? Are you an interesting read? Are you a thriller, a romance novel? It's the story that you write word for word, page to page, letter to letter.

You have the power to write your own destiny and be with someone who will lift you up, not drag you down. You decide.

You have the power to write what comes next, it's your book, remember you have the pen. You decide what to write. What have you written today? Have you spent the day making things happen or have you wasted a chapter. It is something to think about.

TRUE LOVE DOES EXIST

In 1936, King Edward VIII abdicated his throne and stood down as king so that he could marry Wallis Simpson, the woman he loved. He was frozen out of the royal family because of his choice to marry her. This man turned his back on being king because it wouldn't allow him to be with Wallis. He married Wallis and the two grew old together. His decision rocked a nation.

True love exists around us every day, in our friends, our children, and our parents. If you find the right receptor, your red wolf, love can be the most magical thing in the world. I witnessed true love when I saw my sister putting together a scrapbook for her fiancé the night before their wedding. I witnessed true love with my friends and family who have stood by me through the light and the dark times. I feel true love when I look at my son.

Look at Stephen Hawking's wife, Jane Wilde. A film was made on their lives, and it inspired me. She was a remarkable woman. Even with the knowledge Stephen would end up in a wheelchair with a limited life expectancy, she said, "I do," and stood by him for thirty years. Could you?

True love exists, but just as we find in the ocean, there are some beautiful creatures, and there are some sharks. Through life experience we can see a shark coming a mile away. Have faith in love, and dream of your Mr. Right. He is out there, probably sitting with a friend and having a discussion wondering where you are. I have spent Christmas alone. I have rocked up to endless functions and stood alone. I have felt embarrassed when a relationship didn't work out, when I was let down. I have felt lonely. I have felt so lonely at times that I questioned if I would meet Mr. Right one day. My friends have told me that I'm too fussy and need to lower my expectations. In my core, there is a fire in me that believes in everything I have written.

I can say that to get where I am today was worth every tear I have shed and every heartbreak I have endured. Given the choice, I wouldn't change a thing. Don't lose heart. Don't lower your expectations. Have faith. You are not alone. Your book is just different—your chapter will come.

Just as the seasons change, you will have your summer—even though it feels like your winter is going on forever.

WHAT DO MEN REALLY WANT IN A WOMAN?

While writing this book, I asked over a five hundred men what their top three most attractive qualities were in women. There were certain qualities that always came up: The first was a sense of humour. The second was loyalty. The third was confidence. Also popular were independence and intelligence. Seldom did appearance come up, which was really refreshing. So why do we all give so much importance to it? Food for thought, isn't it? It reinforces the power of a soul connection.

Of course attraction is important but the real glue between people is not external. I advocate investing in yourself and your appearance because it's like mowing your lawn, we want our gardens to be nice, not overgrown and untidy. I think we should take pride in our appearance, but as we have learned love goes deeper. Love knows you may not have a perfectly symmetrical lawn, but loves it anyway. The message is none of us are perfect. I have a friend who adores people with large noses. She finds that attractive. She tells me it adds character to a person. What people really want is someone to make them laugh, a best friend. You may have a bumpy lawn but someone will love your bumpy lawn. Don't compare yourself to others. You are unique and it is sometimes the things that aren't perfect that people find the most attractive.

I have a male friend who prefers large women he is not attracted to slimmer girls. Society dictates that being slim is more attractive. This is simply not true. The modeling world is now embracing the larger lady, and rightly so. Don't ever measure being attractive solely on physical appearance. No matter what shape or size you are. You are you for a reason and that's what makes attraction so special. For many people they will prefer a house with a garden but some they'd opt for an apartment. Although the house with a garden may appear the most popular choice, some just won't find that appealing. It's the same with people. Attraction is complex embrace the complexities and difference about yourself.

WOMEN NEED TO STICK TOGETHER

My dad once said to me that if you can count more than two true friends on your hand at the end of your life, you are lucky—if you count five, you are a liar. I believe this is true. This needs to change. Women need to look out for each other. Women need to tell the married man to get lost. They need to look out for the new girlfriend if there is a need. They need to tell their friends when they look good, give them confidence, and build up their self-esteem. They need to be honest with friends and speak up if a friend is with a guy who they know is a jerk. The other woman doesn't have to be the enemy. Women have the power. Women run governments they bear children. Women shouldn't be crying into their pillows over men. The sharks need outing. If women stopped looking at other women as competition and were inspired by them instead, the world of dating would be far more fun. Have your girls' backs.

WORZEL GUMMIDGE

Remember the British children's television series *Worzel Gummidge*? For those who don't remember, it was about a scarecrow that came to life when no one was around. Worzel would have different heads that he could physically take off. The different heads changed his persona. For example, one was a studious Worzel, and one was a funny Worzel.

When you step out of that door to go on a date, the only head you should wear is your own. Be yourself, because if you try to be something you're not or someone you're not, you're only cheating yourself. In time, you will be found out. If you try to pretend that you love the outdoors when you really love being a couch potato, he will find out in time. In other areas of our life, taking on different personas is necessary and can be productive, but with affairs of the heart, be yourself.

A friend of mine met a lovely guy. They got along great while they were dating. He had a huge dog, which was his life. My friend wasn't the biggest dog lover but pretended that she was. She would swoon over the dog when she came in contact with it.

The more time the two of them spent together, the more some things started to bother her. He was tied to being at home most of the time because of the dog, and they couldn't go away for romantic weekends as a result. The dog had its own sofa and wasn't very well trained. My friend would walk in the house, dressed to the nines, and the dog would jump up, mucking her clothes.

For her birthday, she booked a romantic weekend away, and the dog had to come too. It was okay when the dog was running up and down during a long country walk, but when they sat down for some lunch, the dog would whine throughout the meal. My friend said she didn't know if she could live with the dog, and her boyfriend wasn't about to get rid of it—the dog had its own sofa for god's sake!

This is what happens when we aren't honest and true to ourselves. Before we know it, we are compromising so much that we end up becoming unhappy. We end up back at the beginning and have to try to find ourselves again.

Is a guy worth giving up who you are, what you like, and what makes you happy?

Another friend's partner is obsessed with computer games. For me, that is a big no. It may seem like a small thing, however, when you're spending Sunday afternoons alone, coming in second to a PlayStation 3, and others are on the top of the Eiffel Tower drinking champagne or walking the moors with their dream guys, you may think twice!

Again, reading the signs could save you years on that motorway.

I avoid cyclists. I know I will be spending weekends alone while they are on quests for new cycling routes. I also avoid big gym goers. I like to keep fit, but it's about a balance. People who spend every day in the gym don't have the kind of balance that I am looking for. I am honest with myself, and I'm aware of compatibility. Some women will love dating a cyclist and may cycle themselves so that they will be better suited.

It's about looking at the bigger picture—not just his pictures.

IT'S OKAY TO BE SINGLE

This is something I feel strongly about. In this book I have talked about why waiting for the right guy to come along is so important. It's the social pressure that single people feel that pushes them into the arms of the wrong relationship. This has to change. I have felt this firsthand. I have had the "Are you still single?" comments and felt almost embarrassed. The question is always asked rhetorically; they already know the answer, and it's almost a veiled insult. Not anymore—there is a new kid in town.

I hope the stories I have shared will empower other single people to hang in there. It is better than okay to be single—it is empowering to say you are single because you haven't met the right person who makes you not want to be single. Being single can be a lot of fun, and, let's face it, you could wake up tomorrow and meet the most amazing person. Anything is possible when you are single. There are no shackles tying you to a place; you are free to do what you want to do. Embrace it, because when the right guy does come along, you will look back and wish you'd had had more fun with it. If just one person's attitude changes toward one single person, my work is done.

I have had some dark times being single, but I wouldn't change them. There is a famous singer who said that she is now struggles for new material for songs because she is in a good place and happy. If I hadn't had all these experiences and been exposed to all these situations, I would have never written this book. Through pain, through dark times, we grow. The most amazing things can happen. Turn the dark times around, because, as you have witnessed, good things come from them. If I hadn't felt so alone at times—and so judged—I may have not felt so compelled to help others who were in the same boat.

I listened to a woman's story at a conference, she became paralyzed after being knocked off her bike. This woman was extremely active prior to her accident. She went on to complete a marathon she didn't allow her disability to temper her spirit. I sat listening to her in sheer admiration, she wasn't bitter or angry and embraced life. She sat in front of hundreds of women and said she wouldn't change her accident. Through this tragedy she had met some amazing people and experienced so much love and help which gave her faith in humanity. No matter how bad your situation may seem, you can turn the bad cards you're dealt in to the best hand you could have ever wished for.

CINDERELLA SLIPPER

We all remember the story of Cinderella's two ugly sisters who try on the glass slipper. They try so hard to squash a foot into the slipper to make it fit. This is like relationships: when you find the right relationship, the shoe fits. Every inch is tailored to fit you perfectly.

Someone close to me went through a very tough time with one particular man. She had been having a long-term affair, hoping that one day he would leave his wife. Two years had elapsed, and he hadn't left. In an effort to forget him, she got herself back in the dating scene and tried to move on.

She has always been the life and soul of any party, and I know instinctively when she is happy with someone.

Feeling low and rejected, she met someone new. He was lovely and very sensible. However, I observed them together and knew she was trying to make him fit. This guy wouldn't hurt her. He treated her very well, but he didn't set her world on fire. Because she was in a fragile place, she went for the teacup ride. This guy wasn't going to hurt her or let her down, so it seemed like a good move.

One night they gave me a lift home. It was all very serious and adult—so not her. I said my good-byes and watched her drive off into the distance. My heart sank; I knew that she was trying to make him fit.

This was a classic example of buying what was available at the time and not waiting for the right person to come along. Jumping straight into a new relationship seems like a good distraction, but looking for someone else to help distract you or heal you is not the way to get over someone. You have to do the work; it's hard but necessary. Deep down, we all know when we are trying to make someone fit. We list the good points—"he's nice," "has a good job," "treats me really well." Of course, these are all lovely qualities, but are they enough? When you meet the right person, you don't need to come up with reasons why you are with him. And you don't need to convince your friends and, more importantly, yourself, that he's right for you. I have listened to women try to convince me they are with the right guy. Look out for it. Are you trying to make him fit because you are scared of being alone? Are you knocking on the door of thirty or another milestone of your own choosing and feeling pressured to settle down? Is it just that you know he won't hurt you? These are not reasons for you to be with someone. It's called settling, and if you want to just settle for second best, then go on making excuses.

NEVER SHOW A MAN YOU FEEL THREATENED BY ANOTHER WOMAN

I gave some advice to a friend. Her partner would constantly try to wind her up and make her jealous, mostly through the women he worked with. She was constantly coming to me, telling me tales of how he was obsessing over the women in his job. This turned my friend into someone she didn't want to be. She became very insecure and obsessive, which was a direct result of the way he treated her.

It is important to note here that her relationship with this man had an unhealthy dynamic. He was always told that he was "punching above his weight," that my friend was out of his league. Others made gestures to her as if to say, "How did he get a woman like you?" It was clear that he loved my friend, but he was quite insecure about himself. When she would get angry, he felt it confirmed her love for him, so he created scenarios to boost his own ego. I don't think he was quite aware of how much this was upsetting my friend.

One night, on February 13, I had a frantic phone call. My friend was raging. When she finally calmed down, she explained that there were two bottles of wine in the fridge—two bottles of her favourite wine, might I add. My friend realised that one of the bottles was for a lady that her partner worked with. He had said that he was going to buy her one for helping him with a meeting at work the week before. Conveniently, he had bought two of the same bottle, and my friend knew instantly that he was going to provide it to this lady at work the following day. But the next day was not just any day—it was Valentine's Day!

This was the point where my friend needed a tool bag of skills to navigate the situation. Ever heard the expression "Do what you always did, get what you always got"? Well, my friend's partner was expecting her to see the wine. He wanted her to go ballistic so that he could make her out to be a psycho. But no, I told her to remain calm and simply ask her partner why there were two bottles of her favourite wine. Perhaps there was a "buy one, get one free" offer? She was under strict instructions not to be mad at him but to simply ask. I told her not to give any attention to it and simply say, "If it is for Amy, I think giving it her tomorrow is a little inappropriate. Why don't you give it her on Monday?"

The result was as I had predicted. He was dumbfounded by her response, and he tried to create an argument saying, "I just won't give her wine at all!" My friend remained calm, and the calmer she was, the more dumbfounded he was.

Men will use other women to make you feel jealous and insecure. The secret is, even if you feel terribly insecure, don't ever let him know that. You will make the other woman appear so much more attractive by giving it attention. If a woman walks into a room when you're on a date and you think, "Wow, I hope he doesn't see her!" don't flinch. Remain unaffected and don't give it any attention. You will be amazed how well it works. By reacting and being jealous, you are saying that that woman is better than you, and you are suggesting that you are worried. No, you are not. Master the art of self-belief.

My friend was amazed at the reaction she got, and the dynamics changed overnight. The fact she agreed for him to give the girl the wine sent a clear message: this girl does not threaten me. His attention quickly changed from the other women to her.

If you are out with a guy and he is constantly looking at other women, chances are he is doing it for one of two reasons: because he is not that interested in you or to get a reaction from you. Men use this tactic to make women feel insecure or to see how they react. Want to make a woman appear more attractive? React. Get insecure. Yell at him for looking at her. Want to make yourself more attractive? Give it no attention whatsoever. If he continues to do it, don't bother with him again.

WHY DOESN'T HE REPLY?

This topic must be the most talked-about topic among women. Why has he not replied? From my experience of observing men and listening to their reasons, I have compiled the following list.

1. Something has happened. He's in hospital, busy with work, or unable to reply for some genuine reason.
2. He's just not interested. Simple—no further explanation required.
3. He is going into avoidance because you have put pressure on him to make a decision or because you have argued with him. He is ignoring you as he doesn't want to deal with the issue.
4. He is doing it to get your attention. He is trying to play it cool as he really does like you.

I have heard men say that they don't want to appear to be too eager so they don't reply straight away; they do exactly what we do. It's a known tactic with both men and women; however, when you are on the receiving end it can be very frustrating, but just think about why. If a guy is waiting before he replies, chances are that he likes you and is making a conscious effort to get your attention.

So if you find yourself waiting for a reply, think about it. Why wouldn't he reply? There is almost always a reason.

WAX AND POLISH

This is a concept that I feel is the key thing with all relationships, be they with lovers or friends. Have you ever waxed a car or polished your shoes? The first step is to apply a thick layer of wax, which immediately dulls the car or boot you are polishing. Then comes the buffing, which creates the shine.

I apply this to people. Some people dull you down—they bring out your insecurities, and they bring your worst traits to the surface. They can wax you so much that you lose your shine; you lose who you are. Then there are the polishers. They bring out your best qualities, they cradle your insecurities and allow you to shine and sparkle like you should.

A friend of mine had a boyfriend who is a waxer. Her partner would constantly put her down, often in very subtle ways that would almost go unnoticed. He would say things like, "You look like a banana in that dress," but he would follow up by saying that he was only joking. My friend, wearing a yellow dress with black shoes, would lose her confidence, and she would change her outfit. He had planted a seed.

Another example of his behaviour was the way he responded to her aspirations. When she spoke to him about going for promotion, he would laugh and say, "You can't even manage yourself, let alone a team!" Those kinds of comments, over time, get under people's skin, but that is the waxers intention. He wanted to knock her confidence. He didn't want her to get promoted; he was insecure, and he wanted her beneath him.

This behaviour doesn't just apply to relationships with men—it goes for your friends as well. I noticed that when I started moving forward and being successful, I started losing friends. Some people would find reasons not to be my friend. I also noticed waxers when I talked about writing a book: the polishers would encourage me; the waxers would make sarcastic negative comments.

It is so important to surround yourself with polishers, people who support you, who want you to be better and make something of your life. Those are the friends who tell you when you look nice and boost your confidence. They are the ones who will push you to reach your goals. We all need support and encouragement. Make your framework solid by being around positive people who are going where you're going.

You will outgrow people in life. The facts are that waxers don't want people to succeed—they don't want others to be confident. They don't want others moving forward and leaving them behind.

Look out for the waxers and polishers in your life. Think about people around you. More importantly, are you a waxer? Or are you a polisher? It's your choice.

Remember, when you polish something, you can see your own reflection. You get something back—knowing you're a secure, good person. When you wax, there's no reflection; there's nothing but negativity.

THE BIG R

The big *R* is the term I use for when we are rejected. Rejection does funny things to people. Is there a time that you were rejected? Think about how it made you feel.

A friend of mine was seeing a guy. She wasn't really that interested in him until he presented the big *R* card! Within minutes, he had turned from someone she wasn't really that bothered about to the most important guy in the world. I remember having discussions with her about him, and she didn't even really fancy him. But now he appeared so much more attractive.

Rejection has a big effect on everyone. It plays tricks with your mind. Even if you don't really like a guy, if he stops giving you attention, you notice it; it gets your attention.

I bring this up because it's important to understand why it has bothered you. Let's go back to my friend. She didn't really fancy this guy, but now he had her hooked.

Remember this when you get the big *R*. Rejection isn't nice. Everyone wants to be wanted, and, rejection can really play tricks with your mind.

This even affects people who are getting divorced. Sometimes, when it has been one partner's choice to end the relationship, he or she will struggle when the other partner accepts it and starts moving on. All of a sudden, that partner will appear attractive again. This is all temporary.

When confronted with rejection, try to play the scenario back in your mind. If the change had been your choice and you rejected the other person, would you still feel the same way? I'm guessing not. We always remember the good things about someone when a relationship ends. Remind yourself of how you felt when you were *with* them, not how you feel without them.

DON'T FISH WITH A FISH ON THE END OF YOUR ROD

This concept is for those who start to seek out a new relationship whilst they are already in one. How are you going to meet Mr. Right when you are living with Mr. Wrong? Have you ever heard the saying, "There are plenty more fish in the sea"? This is true, but a fisherman doesn't go fishing with a fish already on their hook. What would they achieve by doing that other than wasting their time or losing the fish they already have on their rod.

The same thing applies to people who are unhappy in their relationship and start looking for other potential partners whilst they are still with someone. Have you ever been in a relationship and found yourself actively seeking out men/women? Perhaps sat in a bar looking around to see if anyone catches your eye, you find yourself disappointed when you go out and you don't see anyone you are attracted to.

If you ever find yourself doing this, then you need to take a moment to reflect and ask yourself why. People who are in committed relationships do not focus their attention on other men. I know so many people who have found themselves in this situation. If you find yourself wanting to get your fishing rod back out, it would make sense to remove the fish you already have before you start trying to catch a new one!

Do you have girlfriends who, by their own admission, know they aren't with the right guy but stay in a relationship because it's easier than being alone? We all know someone in that position. Remember, being single and available opens doors for new opportunities. You are less likely to get out and actively try to meet new people if you are already in a relationship. Flat route or climb? Your choice.

DON'T LET THEM PUT YOU IN A BOX

I mentioned earlier I had had my teeth straightened. At the same time, I had them whitened. I was told by my dentist to drink through a straw while going through the process. I work in a professional organisation, and drinking through a straw just wasn't done! I had a choice: Did I look after my teeth and drink through a straw? Or did I conform in order to fit in.

I decided to drink though a straw. I got comments like "You're a weirdo," or "Who drinks through a straw?"—said in the nicest possible way, of course!

It was simple. I had a choice. Should I conform and behave how others wanted me to? Or should I carry on regardless? I carried on regardless because I felt that my own opinion was more important. Yes, they called me weird, but I let them.

I often get comments like "You need to settle down and find someone." Why should I? So that I will fit in with everyone else? No, I think we have come to an age where people are starting to say no. They won't try to fit in the box that others are trying to put them in.

I embrace doing what is right for me regardless of what people think. The more that people start to be themselves and stop worrying about being liked and fitting in, the better the world will be and the happier people will be. Don't let society put you in a box. Have conviction in yourself and in everything you do. All it takes is one person to have the confidence, not to follow the crowd, and others will feel empowered to follow. It's called being yourself, why is it so hard?

Remember being yourself acts as a filter, the people who are worth having in your life will remain, the rest will be filtered out. The best way to find your soul mate is by being yourself. If you are not being yourself, how can you attract the person that is truly right for you?

Don't let them put you in a box, boxes are not for the living.

OWN IT

I have spoken to thousands of men and women, and one thing that is universally attractive to everyone is confidence. Like I have said, I am a little different. I have been called eccentric. At first, I was a little uncomfortable with that word; I imagined a person who was walking around wearing psychedelic pants! Then I thought about it. I did drink through a straw. I was different! So I decided to own it. Yes, I am a little eccentric, and I love it!

The day I faced who I was and owned it was the day I was free. It's amazing to see people's reaction when you own it. In my experience, people struggle with confident people. It is their way of trying to control you, trying to make you conform, to put you in box so that you're not a threat.

The next time someone says something to you about how you are, own it, and say, "Yes, I am, and I wouldn't want it any other way. How boring would life be if we all were the same?" Watch their response.

Have the confidence to let people mock you. Have the confidence to own who you are. The key ingredient to life is having confidence in yourself. Master that, and the rest will fall into place.

PERSONAL DATE NIGHT

I have talked about dating and relationships, but the most important relationship starts with the one you have with yourself. Make time at least once a week to have time for you—pamper yourself, do your nails, or read a book. Do things that make you happy. Being happy starts with *you* being happy with *you*.

My niece loves nothing more than a hot bubble bath, lighting candles and listening to some relaxing music. She does this every night without fail. I secretly think she is part mermaid! She takes time out for herself and says she likes to reflect on her life and what she has taken from her day.

I believe this is something we all need to do. Take time to take our protective armor off, the same way we take our clothes off, to get clean from the day we've had. We can all be in denial about problems in our life, however facing them is so important. Take time to read the road signs in your life, it may be a problem you're avoiding addressing. Whatever it may be, it's better to deal with it, and reflect, than file it in the hope it will go away.

I enjoy a long walk in the country side, I try and do this at least once a week. I am a better version of me when I meet my own wants and needs. Learn to understand what makes you perform better. Some like to relax with a glass of wine, others may enjoy going for a massage.

Imagine yourself as a car, if you don't take care of your engine eventually problems will arise. Be one step ahead by learning what makes you run effectively. If you take time out, your relationships with others can only benefit. My friend is always in a good mood after going for a run, she knows this is the oil and water in her engine. Her partner knows if she doesn't get time to do this she becomes agitated and short tempered.

Also take the time to clean out your closet, by that I mean address your issues and worries as they arise, don't let that filling cabinet get too full!

We have needs on all different levels, emotional, social, physical, intellectual and many more. Paying attention to these needs allows us to have healthier, happier relationships. As with my friend she knows meeting her physical needs makes her more fun to be around.

Take time to list the things that make you happy. Whatever it is that you enjoy, *make a date in your diary with yourself.*

"Dress yourself top to toe in self-esteem"

DRESS YOURSELF TOP TO TOE IN SELF-ESTEEM

This is my final concept, and it is the one that is the most important to me. When you get dressed every day you put on clothes, shoes, makeup, and perfume. The one thing you should never leave the house without is your self-esteem. I use the idea of dressing from head to toe in self-esteem because it is the most attractive, most beautiful trait a person can have.

Every time you leave the house, think to yourself, "I'm dressed in self-esteem. I won't settle for second best. I won't allow people to treat me poorly or with disrespect. I won't give my time to people who don't value me."

Surround yourself with positive people who are polishers not waxers. This applies to every relationship you have, be it with friends or colleagues. If you apply this concept you will notice your relationships change, and you will be perceived differently by others.

Never mind dripping in bling and diamonds—be dripping in self-respect and self-esteem, and you will shine far brighter than any diamond.

THE CHECKLIST

All my concepts are summarised below. Read them, and keep reminding yourself how important it is to have confidence in yourself.

Being Single

Remember, you are not alone. Millions of people enjoy being single. You can meet anyone and do anything when you are single. Your ex has most probably done you a huge favour, although you might not know it yet. When one door closes another one opens!

Frankenstein's Concept

If it's dead, let it go. Don't stay. As we have explored, it can create a monster in you and in your partner. Arguments can lead to violence when emotions are high.

Selling Your House

Give yourself a makeover. Treat yourself to that new dress. You deserve it. Be it taking up a new sport or learning a new language, do something to invest in you.

Invest in Your Inner Self

If we break our leg and don't go for treatment, we may never be able to walk again. It's the same with our mental health—if neglected, the damage can be for life. Is it time to declutter your mind, clear out some old baggage?

Observe What You Attract

Take time to think about your previous relationships. Is there a pattern emerging? Take time to analyse all your relationships, are they positive or negative? Do you attract the undesirables! Is it time to look at why? Remember understanding your behaviour is powerful and can change your future relationships.

The Empty Basket

Have lots of eggs in your basket. By eggs, I mean options. Always have lots of options, hobbies, and interests—and lots of dates!

Living in Reverse

Don't live in the past. Don't dwell on the past. Move forward in everything you do. Tomorrow is another day.

Have a Destination

If you don't know what you want, how can you get it? Start today. Write down your future goals and wants. Don't compromise, don't limit yourself and be clear in your mind about where you want to be. If you ask a child what it wants to be, it will have no limitations. Why should that change as an adult? The sky is the limit.

Don't Look for Bread in the Meat Aisle

Do your research. When you know what you want, the next step is putting yourself in the right place at the right time.

Helpful Guidelines

These seven guidelines add structure to dating and help you avoid pitfalls.

Get the Right Exposure

You could have the most beautiful house up for sale, but what if it's not advertised anywhere? How can you expect it to sell? Get out there, and give yourself maximum exposure. Exposure in the right places!

Never Conform

Have the confidence to not follow the crowd. Do what is right for you. It could save you years of being in the wrong relationship with the wrong person. Remember it takes one person to have the courage not to follow the crowd for others to have the confidence to follow. Be true to yourself.

Are You Choosing between Two Guys?

If you like two people and can't decide which to choose, neither one is right. You won't need to deliberate when you meet the right guy. You will just know.

Don't Buy a House without Viewing It

You wouldn't invest time and money into a home without doing your research. It is the same with relationships. Be sure to do your research before you make huge commitments. Look at someone's past, when we buy a new car we always look to see if it has full service history! Someone's morals and values will be a great indication of what and who they are.

Always Go with Your Instinct

Your best friend is your instinct. Listen to it, and use it.

Actions Speak Louder than Words

When in doubt about how someone feels, always look at their actions. They will speak a thousand words.

Be a Friend to Yourself

Turn things around: what you would tell a good friend to do if she was in your position? The next time you think about doing something that you know isn't right or good for you, ask yourself, "Am I being a friend to myself?"

Be a Friend to Others

Don't forget your single friends when you are happy. They need you; look out for them.

The Supply Teacher

Don't be a pushover. Have boundaries; they generate respect.

The Pied Piper Concept

Don't get sucked in by people's false promises. Take a step back. When in doubt, look at peoples actions; they always speak louder than words!

Climb the Hill or Take the Flat Route?

It is your choice. No pain, no gain. Don't take the easy option, and you will always see results.

Teacup Ride or Roller Coaster?

Look out for the safe relationships, and look out for the destructive ones. You now have a title to refer to these kinds of relationships. Are you on a teacup ride? Have fun with it.

The Power of No Reply

This is a very powerful tool and highly effective. If someone is treating you with disrespect, try this tactic. You will be amazed at how well this works.

Leading Lady or Chorus?

You should always be the leading lady in your life. Is it time to make changes?

Think like a Ten

No further explanation required. You are going to be you for a very long time. Maybe it is time to learn to love yourself. Concentrate on your good points, and use the power of positive thinking.

Don't be the Empty Restaurant

Have fun with this. Don't be available all of the time. It's like trying to get in at the most exclusive restaurant you know—you need to book in advance. Make people learn to book in advance with you.

Money Doesn't Make You Better

Don't be intimidated by wealth and status. Whenever you meet someone, take money off the table. Look at who he or she is as a person. Let that be your guide. What can he/she bring to the table?

Don't Show the Whole Film Only the Trailer

Don't tell your life story on the first date. Show people snippets of who you are so they will want to watch the whole movie.

Tennis Game

Let your interactions be like tennis—back and forth. Don't hijack the conversation. Allow other people to talk about themselves too.

Never Show Your Hand

In the beginning, don't tell people exactly how you feel. Keep them guessing. It keeps the element of surprise and keeps things exciting and interesting. Let him or her wonder a little.

The Ballerina Concept

Look out for the people who are constantly on their toes, trying to impress their partner and constantly worrying and feeling insecure.

Never Give Up Your Life for a Man

Never lose who you are or give up your friends or life for someone else. It is a long way back to find yourself, and some friendships can never be found again.

Monkey See, Monkey Do

What's good for the goose is good for the gander—mirror behaviour. I mean this in the most lighthearted way. If he has a weekend away with the boys, you have a weekend away with the girls.

Flip the Coin

Don't let anyone make you feel insecure. If a guy tries to do this, show him a mirror—do it back. Sometimes the best way to show someone is by letting them see how it feels.

Beauty Is in the Eye of the Beholder

Please remember this concept, and keep it in mind. There is someone out there for everyone. You don't need to look like a supermodel to find your Mr. Right.

Fallback Girl

Don't be anyone's fallback girl. If you are getting calls late at night to be the booty call, alarm bells should start ringing. If you have been dating for a long time and you still haven't met friends and family, again, red flag. This looks like a No Entry sign to me! Read the signs.

Limbo Land

Don't wait around for someone else to make decisions. Get a ticket out of limbo land. If you are being messed around and don't know where you stand, you are in limbo. You can wait around for someone to make decisions for you, or you can take control of the situation and make decisions yourself.

Indicate, Mirror, Signal, Manoeuvre

Think about how you come across. What messages are you sending with your body language? Are you approachable?

Unplug the Source

If someone is causing you pain, unplug them. Remove yourself from the source of the pain. If you got badly sunburned, you wouldn't go back out in the sun the next day. You would stay away from the sun and protect yourself. It's no different with emotional pain. Think about the damage you are doing to your emotional well-being.

Reason, Season, or Lifetime?

Remember, relationships come and go. Just because some are short-lived doesn't mean they are any less special or less important than the ones that last a lifetime. Learn from all your relationships. Let them be a mirror for who you are.

Red Wolf

You are unique; not everyone will get you. It may take you longer to meet your soul mate because you have to find your match. Don't think that just because you have been single awhile that there is something wrong with you. One of my male friends was single for seven years. He is now married with a daughter and incredibly happy. Your book is just different. Have faith.

A Good Gambler Knows When to Quit

The message is, know when to cash in your chips, know when it's time to stop rolling the dice. It's important to stand your ground in relationships but it's equally important to know when to let something go. Learn to let the small things go.

Living in the Moment

Don't worry too much about next week or next year. Don't spend your time worrying about if you might get hurt in a relationship—it takes away the shine. Live in the moment, and enjoy. Don't be planning how you will cope with the ending before you've even begun!

The Emperor's New Clothes

Remember the story of the emperor who went along with the ridiculous story of his imaginary new clothes? If something sounds too good to be true, it most probably is. If most of your friends are telling you that your partner is an idiot, there is a reason. Don't agree or compromise in order to fit in.

Do We Ever Really Know Someone?

Look at someone's past. It will usually be a good indicator of what kind of person he or she is. Read the road signs. If something doesn't add up, ask yourself why. Look at the MOT certificates! Have they passed, are they reliable.

Life is Short

All we have and all we can be sure of is this moment, this day. Life can be taken in a heartbeat, so live your life to its fullest. Make that bucket list.

Find the Right Receptor

If you find the right receptor, things just work. Just like plugging the right plug into the right socket. When we are abroad, our plugs don't work—they just don't fit. Some people won't fit just right with you, but when you find the right receptor, you can be yourself, and it just works.

Does He Have Your Manual?

This is the same as with good friends—they know how you think, they know when you are down, and they know what makes you laugh. It will feel like he has your instruction manual, because he will know you so well, and it will be effortless.

If You Look Too Hard, You Don't Find

Make a life, and the rest will follow. Having a balance with all things is the key.

What Book Are You?

At the end of your life, if someone were to write a book about you, what book would you be? Be an interesting read. Remember you have are writing the pages of your own book.

True Love Does Exist

True love does exist, and it can move mountains. Don't ever lose faith in love.

What Do Men Really Want in a Woman?

It's seldom about how we look; it's about how we think. That is within your control, and being yourself is the key.

Women Need to Stick Together

Women are amazing creations. Have your girls' backs.

Worzel Gummidge

In affairs of the heart, be yourself. If you don't, the only person you are cheating is yourself. Have confidence that someone will like you for you. You will know you were true to yourself, and the next date might just be your red wolf.

It's Okay to Be Single

It is more than okay to be single—remember the stories about women who tried to conform and fit in. Years of their lives were wasted being unhappy.

Cinderella's Slipper

Don't try to make the shoe fit. Be honest with yourself. Is he the right guy for you?

Never Show a Man You Feel Threatened by Another Woman

If you display jealousy or insecurity, you are saying "I am not good enough. I am insecure." Is that the message you want to give? It is normal to feel jealousy however it's how we deal with it that makes the difference. When you feel jealous remind yourself, there is only one you, and no one else can compare to you!

Why Doesn't He Reply?

If he hasn't replied, there will always be a reason. Don't jump to conclusions straight away. Eventually, you will find out the reason, but it's not always a bad thing.

Wax and Polish

Surround yourself with people who make you feel good and bring out the best in you—the polishers. Look out for the waxers; they will always try to knock you down.

The Big *R*

Rejection does funny things to people. If you have been rejected, keep reminding yourself of how you felt when you were with him, not without him. You might look back with rose-tinted glasses if you have been rejected. It's just life. Watch for the signs, move forward and take another road instead.

Don't Fish with a Fish on the End of Your Rod

Don't date that guy just for the sake of it. Have fun and experience dating. However, if you are spending time with someone when you know there is no future, chances are you are less likely to put yourself out there to meet the right person. Remember if you want to get your fishing rod back out, remove the fish you already have from the end of your rod!

Don't Let Them Put You in a Box

Don't let people stop you from being who you are. Never conform to fit in. The world is changing, we have never been so forward thinking as a generation. Remember the people in life who didn't conform such as Robin Hood. He was persecuted in this lifetime but sowed the seeds of change for the next generation. Give people the courage to be themselves be Robin Hood who never conformed.

Own It

Own who you are, and wear it with pride. Those who don't like it are no loss to you. It's better to have real friends than pretend ones. Use owing it as your sieve, filter out those who are not worthy. The people worth being around are those who encourage you to be who you are not ridicule you for it.

Personal Date Night

Do something once a week just for you: read that book, have a facial, get your nails done. Make time for just you.

Dress Yourself Top to Toe in Self-Esteem

Before you step out of the house, be sure you are dressed head to toe in self-esteem. You will shine far brighter than any diamond.

CONCLUSION

Keep reading over this book. Remind yourself of each concept. You now have a fun way to describe certain behaviours. Look out for the ballerinas and the teacups. Keep exercising your mind the same way you do your body.

Some men like a challenge. Most men love a chase. It is so much fun playing hard to get, and men will feel like they have found someone worth waiting for. The harder you are to attain, the more men will think you are worth fighting for, and they will go to greater lengths to see you again.

Make them work for your time. In fact, make it impossible to see you all the time. If they want you, they will make an effort to be in your company. It is easy to forget, to revert back to old behaviours. Keep practicing positive thinking.

Women are wonderful creatures. We need to be looked after and loved. It's what we deserve. Act like a doormat, and you will be one. Think like a ten, and you will be a treated like a ten.

Are good men hard to find? Not really. There are good things in all men; they just choose who they want to be a good man for. The answer lies with you. Are you going to be a yes girl, the pushover who allows a man to walk all over you? The choice is yours. Men love a girl who has an opinion, who will put them in their place when needed.

Walking away from people we love is incredibly difficult, but if they aren't treating you how you deserve to be treated, wait for someone who will. I met someone who I absolutely adored. He made me laugh like no one else, and being in his company was magic. Although I'm sure he felt the same way, he wasn't treating me how I deserved to be treated. I could live without the laughter, but the one thing I absolutely couldn't live without was respect. Climb or flat route? I choose climb every time.

Remember, when someone loves you, he wants to be with you, not without you. I always say to my girlfriends, if he is not knocking on your door making an effort he is simply just not worth it. We can all get involved with someone who isn't treating us right, it's having the confidence to take the exit. Be honest with yourself, don't make excuses for someone's behaviour. Remember it could cost you years on the motorway.

Investing in your inner self is like navigating around an iceberg. You can see your problems and challenges before you hit them. Knowing why you attract certain types of people is powerful stuff. Understanding yourself is like understanding how a high performance car operates. You get the best performance out of you.

Before you consider any new relationship clean your canvas, you will see a dramatic change within all your relationships if you take the time to do this. Know yourself and have a destination. The most valuable advice I could give you, is learn to date yourself, before you even consider dating someone new.

We are all here on this planet struggling through our own stuff. However, there are signs to guide us. There is help when you need it. There are different routes you can take to get to your destination. If you are true to yourself, you won't go far on the wrong path. If a road is closed, there is always a diversion, there is always a way to get where you want to be. Just remember, on this journey we call life, always read the road signs!

ABOUT THE AUTHOR

Mereda Cruz currently lives in the United Kingdom.